Is That Really You, Lord?

LOREN CUNNINGHAM

with Janice Rogers

KINGSWAY PUBLICATIONS

EASTBOURNE

Printed in Great Britain for
KINGSWAY PUBLICATIONS LTD
Lottbridge Drove, Eastbourne, E. Sussex BN23 6NT by
Richard Clay (The Chaucer Press) Ltd, Bungay, Suffolk.
Typesetting by Nuprint Services Ltd, Harpenden, Herts.

Table of Contents

Acknowledgments

Janice Rogers and I wish to thank the many friends who have made this book possible. Especially, Linda Bond, Lori Bragg, June Coxhead, Katherine Ewing, Jeff Fountain, Sandy Grey, Dodie Gunderson, Becky King, Diane Koppen, Kristen Meidal, Joe Portale, Jim Rogers, Barbara Thompson and Nancy Wade. We also thank the dozens of people who spent hours being interviewed for background information. A special honor and thanks go to our friend John Sherrill for his labor of love in overseeing this project.

A Word about the Supernatural

This is a book about the outright supernatural.

And, I, for one, am ready for it.

When my wife, Elizabeth, and I co-authored some of the early books of the Renewal Movement, (*The Cross and the Switchblade, God's Smuggler, The Hiding Place*) we included accounts of mystery and miracle, not because they were sensational but because without them the events we were reporting could not have happened. For the past decade the emphasis in American publishing has shifted somewhat, toward the believer's need for personal commitment and discipline.

But the pendulum is swinging back again, as it always must, between the twin truths of God's initiative and our responsibility. This book by Loren Cunningham is full of startling evidences of God's sovereign activity in our lives today. So inexplicable, in fact, in human terms, were Loren's experiences, that he and his co-author, Janice Rogers, and I made a decision. We went through the manuscript eliminating instances of miraculous guidance that could not be verified by "two or three witnesses," (the Bible's own standard for accuracy).

I include myself in this decision because I acted as editorial consultant on the project, living for weeks at a time on one of the 113 worldwide Youth With A Mission (YWAM) bases, overseeing the writing of the book. It was a new experiment in teaching-by-doing and out of it I feel has come a fine new author, Loren's sister, Janice Rogers. She has done a sensitive job in blending a good narrative with solid teaching on a subject of central importance to every Christian, "How can I learn to recognize the voice of God?"

One problem the three of us never did solve. There were so many superb stories, many of them old YWAM favorites; there were so many people who seemed essential to the narrative; so many teachers who just could not be left out! I finally stepped in as the outsider and made the bound-to-be-unpopular choice. Since we can't tell the whole story—not in a dozen books this length—this sampling will have to represent riches only hinted at here.

So if you already know YWAM don't look for your own favorite memory—it probably won't be here. And if you *don't* already know YWAM, you have an adventure in store! A first look at a God who moves in power in human lives. A God who waits to be invited into yours. . . .

John Sherrill
Chosen Books
Lincoln, Virginia

Chapter One

All That Glitters . . .

I bounded up the wide marble steps of Aunt Sandra's Palm Beach home, settled on the shore of Lake Worth, which she and Uncle George had purchased from a member of the Vanderbilt family. The Florida night was illuminated by floodlights set among tropical foliage and by the golden hue cast from the tall windows of the house. I rang the bell at the double doors. Hawkins, cold and formal as usual, threw the bolt and ushered me into the marble foyer graced with statues and Grecian urns.

"Good evening, Master Loren." Hawkins still called me *Master Loren* even though I was 26 years old! "Mrs. Meehan will join you in the library."

"Thank you, Hawkins. You are looking well."

Hawkins bowed slightly, led me into the library and went to find my aunt. Of all the twenty rooms in Aunt Sandra's winter home, I liked the library best, with its Persian rug and its floor-to-ceiling bookcases, its muted greens and browns. "You'll never belong here, though," I whispered to myself, catching a glimpse of my image in a mirror behind one of the wing-backed chairs. The light hit me at an angle and I could still see the shadow of acne scars left over from my teenage years, so recently behind me. If I had come to live with Aunt Sandra, as she had wanted, I'd have gone to an expensive dermatologist. My hair, wavy and dark brown, did not have that bleached-out look of the usual Palm Beach sun fans. I was fashionably lanky, as was Aunt Sandra, but not for the right reasons I'm afraid; I just had not eaten much on this trip around the world. My eyes fell on a huge illuminated world globe that stood by Uncle George's favorite dark leather chair and for the briefest moment I saw again the strange vision that had been haunting my life for six years now, ever since I was twenty. The vision was of wave upon wave of young people, like myself, missionaries still in their teens and early twenties, marching onto the shores of all the continents of the world. . . . The vision was tantalizing. What brashness made me think it was a mandate from the Lord? A lot of people get "visions." Could mine really be one of those special guiding events that launch a great work for God! If I tried to suggest that to sensible Aunt Sandra I knew it would threaten her.

Aunt Sandra walked in, followed by her dog Gail. "Welcome back, dear!" Aunt Sandra glided across the Persian rug, her quiet grace and elegance a contrast to the boxer who bounded up to me. Aunt Sandra and my father had been raised in the same poor, itinerant preacher's home. Of all the adjectives you could use about their childhoods, elegant was not a candidate.

"It's really good to have you here. George will be home later." Uncle George, I knew, would still be at his club. George Meehan had made his fortune in textiles before settling down to a rhythm of summers in Lake Placid, winters in Palm Beach and autumns and springs in Providence, Rhode Island. My most vivid memory of Uncle George was of seeing him practice golf at the summer mansion by driving a bucketful of balls into the lake. That was Uncle George.

"Loren," Aunt Sandra was saying, "I know you must be exhausted. But first, how about a bedtime snack?" It was a standing joke, my love for the delicacies of their cook. A maid brought the food in and while I ate hungrily and Aunt Sandra nibbled, I told her about my exploratory trip around the world; I'd been trying to understand the meaning of that strange vision of young missionaries. Aunt Sandra was not too interested. She had been so turned off by Christianity during her childhood that now she wanted to leave it behind She listened absently to my story but when I paused she quickly cut in.

"I'm glad for you, Loren," she said, standing. "It's good for young people to get these things out of their systems. We have a *lot* to talk about, but you've come a long way today. We can take it up in the morning."

Making my way upstairs to the large bedroom that had become mine, I knew very well what Aunt Sandra wanted to talk about: a generous offer from Uncle George. Strangely, I didn't look forward to it. I slipped between the carefully-turned-back silk sheets and lay there worrying while the moon's blue shadows moved around the room. Tomorrow I'd have to tell my aunt that the Lord had spoken to me.

I folded my arms behind my head and stared at the dark ceiling. How do you explain to someone who has been hurt already by such pronouncements, that you have heard the voice of God? Before I tried to tell my aunt, I had better be sure I was looking honestly, really honestly, at guidance—including the parts that had turned off Aunt Sandra.

Hearing God's voice had more than once brought me and my family to turning points that changed lives. My dad's father owned a successful laundry in Uvalde, Texas, and was living comfortably when he received what he termed a "call" to preach. He put his business up for sale. "You're a fool, I'll say it outright," said Granddad's brother, to which Granddad replied, "If I heard God right and didn't obey, that's when I'd be the fool."

I have always been intrigued by what happened next. At first Granddad obeyed his call in a part-time fashion, taking a string of jobs in various towns in Texas and preaching on weekends. Then tragedy hit. He and his family were living in San Antonio in 1916 when a dreaded smallpox epidemic broke out. His wife and two sons (there were two young boys and three older girls in the family), were stricken with the terrifying pox. Granddad went to the hospital isolation ward to live with his sick wife and little boys.

For two weeks, Granddad Cunningham maintained his vigil by the beds of his wife and sons. At last the disease seemed to be abating. Granddad got word to the three girls to get everything tidy because soon they'd be coming home.

But then with terrifying swiftness his wife's condition changed. Everyone stood by helplessly as she struggled and weakened and then drew her last breath. The authorities insisted on burying Grandmother immediately, right from the hospital. A few hours later, stunned, weeping, Granddad and the two boys rode home in the same ambulance that was supposed to have brought Grandmother back. The three girls came running out happily.

"Where's Mother?" they asked. When Granddad told them, the oldest girl, Arnette, screamed and ran into the house. The younger girls, Gertrude and Sandra, held each other and cried. But the trauma was not over. That same day health authorities arrived at Granddad's house and announced that mattresses and clothing had to be dragged into the yard and burned. In one day Granddad and his family lost everything but each other. And in a sense they even lost each other, because of what happened next.

Incredibly, Granddad Cunningham announced, not long after the cumulative tragedy, that he was going to start preaching full-time. And here is the part of Granddad's story that gave Aunt Sandra so much trouble. Hearing God is not all that difficult. If we know the Lord, we have already heard His voice—after all it was the inner leading that brought us to Him in the first place. But we can hear His voice once and still miss His best if we don't keep on listening. After the *what* of guidance comes the *when* and the *how*. Granddad obeyed the what of his call—to preach the Gospel—but failed to seek further guidance as to how God wanted him to do that. If he had, maybe the ensuing conflicts would have been far less painful.

Granddad saw himself as a traveling teacher. He couldn't take five children on the road with him so he placed them in different homes—first with relatives, later with farmer friends who took them in for the chores they could do. In those days, if a child had a roof over his head and three meals a day, people reckoned he was being cared for. Granddad's own five reacted to his decision very individually. Two had more or less neutral responses as the years passed. My aunts, Sandra and Arnette, blamed their difficult, tearing childhoods on what they saw as Granddad's foolish call. They decided that they would have nothing at all to do with this kind of Christianity. As soon as they were old enough they each struck out on their own and went into business, determined to make as much money as they possibly could; that was their solution to the loss of mother and home. They succeeded, too. Aunt Arnette did well, but Aunt Sandra had spectacular success, living eventually in three mansions.

And my own father, Tom, the older of the two boys? Incredibly, after a hard upbringing in nine different foster homes, Dad never blamed Granddad for obeying the call to preach. In fact by the time he was seventeen, Dad knew that he, too, had a call. He began to travel with Granddad, holding revival meetings throughout the Southwest.

His decision was followed, as perhaps it usually is, by a challenge. Dad received a rare letter from his oldest sister, Arnette, who was living in Miami.

Dad opened the envelope, pulling out a page of Arnette's angular writing. If he would finish high school, Arnette said, she would pay his way through college so that he could earn an engineering degree. It was a great opportunity. But Dad also knew it would take him away from his calling. He thanked Arnette but told her he couldn't accept.

Arnette's reaction was swift and brutal. "If you are going to tramp through life living off charity with religion as an excuse," she wrote, "I'm through with you!"

The words stung, because they seemed to fit—especially as he started helping Granddad with his meetings. Granddad never graduated to the more comfortable places. He wanted to help the struggling, small groups of people, and often the only things they could give as payment were canned goods or fresh produce or, occasionally, a chicken. In one place, Granddad and Dad ate stewed apples three times a day—without sugar or spice—for two weeks.

After three years of meager fare, Dad was tired of it all. He was nineteen, and although he still considered himself called to preach, he figured he'd wait a while. He left Granddad and found a good job in Oklahoma City working on a construction crew high atop the new Biltmore Hotel.

One day, while he was perched on a six-inch-wide girder on the 24th floor, he watched the giant crane bring up a load of lumber. Suddenly the load swerved straight toward him. He grabbed as the load hit him and in the next instant was dangling in space, desperately holding on while other workmen yelled and hollered. When he got back down, Dad had already made up his mind about one thing: he gave his boss two weeks' notice, then found Granddad, rejoining him for ministry on the road. He never forgot the close brush with death. He had been given a second chance, and this time he was determined to obey God's voice *now,* not at some point in the future when he felt more like it.

Chapter Two

Family Inheritance

When my father, Tom Cunningham, with his square face and wavy black hair, played his guitar and sang in Granddad's meetings, he had no trouble attracting girls.

There was an exception, however.

One day my father and Granddad found themselves in a small Oklahoma town where another family of traveling evangelists was also holding meetings. The Nicholsons' story was colorful. The peppery-witted father, Rufus Nicholson, had been an Oklahoma sharecropper when, at age 40, he gave up his occasional bout of hard drinking, responded to the call of Jesus, piled his family into a covered wagon and began preaching. When Jewell, the third of the Nicholsons' five children, was twelve years old, she was praying on the creek bank late one summer afternoon. Suddenly she heard God speak to her in a clear voice. It didn't surprise Jewell to hear God speaking. People at their camp meetings testified regularly to the experience. Now God was telling her, "I want you to preach My gospel." By the time she was seventeen, Jewell had become one of the regular preachers in the Nicholson clan.

When Tom Cunningham met Jewell Nicholson he was fascinated with the willowy girl with the snapping black eyes and blunt tongue. He began to court her but Jewell was so preoccupied with her own call that at first she paid him scant attention. He persisted for months until Jewell finally warmed up to him. Then he posed the important question and they were married in a simple ceremony in Yellville, Arkansas. Tom had to borrow three dollars for the license.

As newlyweds, my dad and mom began traveling from town to town preaching on the streets or under temporary shelters made of poles overlaid with tree branches which people called "brush arbors."

Those were lean days. Their possessions consisted of an eight-year-old Chevy, a few musical instruments, some clothes and of course their Bibles. With these provisions they fully expected to do the work of God, and do it efficiently.

Which, of course, meant hearing Him with clarity. Both Dad and Mom talked a lot about guidance. They were familiar with the "inner voice," at times quite audible, at other times more of an impression that came fully formed to the mind. They were familiar, too, with hearing Him speak through Scripture, and through dreams and visions. The high purpose of guidance, Dad kept saying, was to tell people about Jesus. "We're fulfilling an urgent command of Jesus Himself," Dad would say when he and Mom talked about the guidance they sought. "The Great Commission, that's the key. 'Go into all the world and preach the Gospel.' " If God did, in fact, commission individuals to the task of going everywhere telling people the Good News, then He would surely guide them.

My parents went wherever they believed God told them to go. They knew snowstorms and freezing rains and living out of the back of automobiles. They lived off whatever the congregation felt like giving them, or the coins folks would throw at their feet if they spoke on the street. But leanness was of small consequence, because all the while they were learning to hear the voice of God and obey. With this sense of adventure in following God's direction, they managed to found three churches, all of which are still in existence today.

In the meantime, Mom and Dad's family was coming along. My sister Phyllis was born in 1933. Two years later I was born in Taft, California, but my earliest memories are of a dusty, desert Arizona town and the sixteen-foot square tent-house with boxes for furniture. I never felt deprived, however, in fact I grew up feeling privileged.

My parents were building a church for a group of sixty parishioners, making with their own hands the adobe bricks which they dried in the sun and used for the walls of the church. They included us in their work and in the process of learning to listen to God. Very early, at the age of six, I had a personal experience in hearing God after a Sunday night meeting and knew for the first time that I belonged to Him. But it was hearing His voice in *everyday* happenings—Monday through Saturday— that meant so much to me! One of these events occurred when I was nine and we were living in Covina, California, an orange tree-filled hamlet 35 miles east of Los Angeles.

It was almost dinner time one evening, and I came running into the front of the house, letting the screen door slam. My sister Phyllis, eleven years old, quickly reminded me with a finger to her lips that our new baby sister, Janice, was asleep in the next room. I wandered into the kitchen where Mom was taking some cornbread out of the oven. I lifted the lid of a big pot on the stove, sniffing the comforting aroma of red beans and salt pork.

"Loren, we're out of milk. Can you go over to the widow's store and buy some?" Mom didn't have any change—just a five-dollar bill. "Now be careful with this. That's our grocery money for the week."

I stuck the bill into the pocket of my jeans, whistled for Teddy, my little brown dog, and headed for the widow's store. It took me a while to get there. I was kicking a can along, and I stopped once or twice to investigate a bottle cap and to pick up a stick to clatter down the neighbors' fences.

I ran up the steps into the widow's store, a living room-turned-grocery, selected two bottles of milk and went to the front desk where the widow lady waited, pencil and pad in hand to total my purchases. But when I reached into my pocket to fish out the bill, my heart stopped. It was gone. I rummaged in the lefthand pocket, the back pockets, my shirt pocket.

"I've lost the money!" I wailed. Leaving the milk behind, I ran back the way I had come, Teddy pumping along behind, searching frantically everywhere I remembered stopping. It was no use. It wasn't anywhere to be found. There was nothing to do but go back and tell Mom I had lost her money.

Mom was still in the kitchen when I came in through the back door closing it ever-so-softly behind me. Mom immediately knew something was wrong. Her face darkened when I told her what I had done—it was such a large loss to us—but she quickly brightened.

"Come, son, let's pray. We'll ask God to show us where that money is."

She stood there in the kitchen, her hand reaching down to my slender shoulder and talked to God. "Lord, you know exactly where that five-dollar bill is hiding. Now we ask You to show us. Speak to our minds, please, for You know that we need that money to feed the family."

Mom stood and waited with her eyes shut. The lid clattered on top of the simmering beans.

Suddenly Mom's grip tightened on my shoulder. "Loren," she said, her voice a fraction lower, "God just told me the money is under a bush." She quickly ducked out the door and I ran to catch up.

The day was deepening to dusk as we retraced my path to the store, inspecting every bush and hedge. It was almost too dark to see when Mom stopped, looking down the street toward a thick evergreen shrub. "Let's try that one!" she said excitedly, heading straight for the shrub. We peered underneath and there, way back at the base of the stubby trunk, was the five-dollar bill.

Sipping tall glasses of milk with our beans and cornbread that night, Mom and I told Phyllis and Dad (and the baby too!) about how God had cared for us that day. We didn't think of these experiences in our family as a sort of school in learning to trust God, but that's exactly what they were.

One February morning three months after the experience with the lost grocery money, we children learned another principle which was to play a continuing role in our lives. We were sitting around the breakfast table when Dad announced that he was going to have to be away from home for a few days. He gave me instructions, since I was ten years old, to take care of the family while he was gone. "I'll be in Springfield, Missouri. That's halfway across the country, but with telephones and all we won't really be out of touch."

It was through the telephone that we got the bad news. Dad

had been stricken with appendicitis. They couldn't operate— peritonitis had probably already set in and with wartime shortages there was no penicillin. It was just a matter of time until he would die.

Mom put the telephone back on the wall and announced that we needed to pray—hard! I crawled behind the couch and stayed there, praying, for hours. Two days passed and Dad continued about the same. We had to hear something from God—some word to help us hold on. Then an event took place which I would never forget.

Three days after we learned of Dad's attack a knock came at the door. I watched as Mother opened the door to the chilly brightness of the February morning. There stood a man from the church. He was the one who reminded me of a funeral director I had once seen, with his drawn features and doleful eyes. He stood there looking more sober than usual, fingering his felt hat, acting as if he were afraid to speak something that was on his mind.

"What is it?" Mother demanded, never shy.

"Sister Cunningham," the gaunt man finally blurted, "God gave me a dream of your husband coming home in a coffin!"

My tongue seemed too big for my mouth. I watched my mom's face. She thought for a moment, then she said,

"Well, sir," Mom's tone was kindly but she spoke with a very distinct firmness, "I do appreciate your coming here to tell me this. Hard as it is, I promise I will ask God if the dream really is from Him. With something this important, He'll tell me Himself won't He?"

It was more of a statement than a question, and with that Mom thanked the gentleman a second time and held open the door. Then she went to prayer. "Is that You, God? I promise to try to accept this man's words if they are really from You. Just let me know, that's all I ask."

Now, Mother had such a believing relationship with her heavenly Father that she fully expected Him to answer her on such an important issue in a fatherly-like manner, with no shadow or doubt. She left it with God and went to bed.

The next morning as we sat down to our breakfast of steaming oatmeal Mom put Jannie into her highchair, then announced that she had some good news. "I had a dream last night," she said to Phylly and me.

We fell silent. "Well?"

"In my dream Dad came home, but it was on a train, and he was wearing his pajamas!"

And that's exactly what happened. We received word that Dad had recovered enough to want to return to California. He had trouble making travel arrangements because of the wartime military priorities, but through friends he managed to get a berth on a Pullman sleeping car. So Dad arrived just as Mom had known he would, on a train, wearing his pajamas. At the station he pulled a pair of trousers over the pajama bottoms. We must have been a sight, walking down the station platform, supporting our still weak, shaky father who shuffled along in his bedroom slippers. Dad didn't care. Neither did we. He was home.

Later, Mom pointed up an important aspect of guidance. "Getting God's leading for someone *else* is tricky," Mom said. "We can hear a confirming voice through another person. But if God has something important to tell you He will speak to you directly."

With this kind of family inheritance, it was not surprising that I, too, should feel the same call to "go into all the world and preach the Gospel." A call, as it turned out, which was to require every bit of knowledge about guidance I possessed.

Chapter Three

The Little Girl Who Changed Our Lives

Often it is only in looking backwards that we catch a glimpse of God's gentle humor as He leads us. I had no idea, for instance, that the stiff, poorly-delivered, ten-minute sermon of a teenage boy would be the subject of my own life for years to come.

That awkward sermon was my own.

I was thirteen years old when we traveled from our new home in West Los Angeles for a reunion with Mom's side of the clan in Springdale, Arkansas.

Dad could be with us for only a few days. But Mom stayed on. She and Dad were both ordained now in the Assemblies of God and my uncle had asked her to hold revival meetings for the youth in his church. (All but one of Mom's relatives were preachers!)

One night after Mom's sermon I knelt at the simple wooden altar rail in the front of my uncle's church. Suddenly I felt as if I were not there but somewhere out in the heavens. Before my eyes, written in bold letters were the words, GO YE INTO ALL THE WORLD AND PREACH THE GOSPEL TO EVERY CREATURE. The Great Commission of Mark 16:15! I opened my eyes but the words were still there. I closed them again and the burning words remained.

There was no doubt in my mind that I was being called to preach. Maybe even to be a missionary, since the words before me said go into "all the world."

I got up from my knees and walked past the other worshipers along the altar and found my mother. I knelt beside her and whispered what had happened to me. Mom looked at me with a big grin and hugged my shoulders. She didn't say much that night, it was the next day that she underlined her real feelings.

"Come with me, son," Mother said in her usual direct way. We walked down to the center of Springdale and found the shoe store. "This young man would like to see a pair of your best shoes," Mom announced. I looked at her in astonishment. My shoes were still serviceable. I wore them to school and to church, but never while out playing with my cousins—we went barefoot any chance we could! Mom looked into my eyes and smiled. "It's to celebrate, Loren. A little something to say how much your dad and I agree with the Bible when it says 'How beautiful on the mountains are the feet of him who brings Good News.'"

My family was delighted to hear my news. "If you are going to preach," said Mom, "there's no time like the present to try your wings!" My uncle agreed and they decided I could take Mom's place at the next Thursday night meeting, a week away.

The thought of getting up in the pulpit and speaking to the browned, sun-wrinkled faces of these Arkansas farmers, filled me with a desire to do my very best. I started to pray about that sermon. For days I asked God to help me find just the right text. The thought came to me, "Preach on the temptations of Christ in the wilderness"—a subject that was to play a very great role for me in my own adventures in guidance.

I felt a bit awkward at the thought of standing in front of grownups and preaching about temptation. All I knew were the temptings of a thirteen-year-old. They were very individualized, as I suppose all temptations are. Oh, I had the normal sexual stirrings of any young teenager but they were not unmanageable. And I'd had my share of boys on the corner lot trying to tempt me to smoke cigarettes; but that seemed just plain silly and I said so and they gave up.

No, as I prayed during that whole week before my first sermon I knew that the "other voices" that tried to lure me away were far subtler, like the urge to keep up with the guys. Not only to keep up, but to excel. Nothing wrong with excelling, but if it begins to twist you then it's a temptation.

And keeping up did tempt me to do things I'd not do normally. Like ride down the center white line of six-lane Olympic Boulevard on my bicycle, cars whizzing by inches away from me and my buddies as we accepted each other's dares. And there were other things I had to do—my light brown hair had to be parted down the side, dipped just right over my forehead and plastered back with lots of Brylcreem. My jeans had to be rolled up at the bottom, my gabardine shirts had to have their sleeves turned up the arm exactly one roll, and on my feet were the Chippewa boots so esteemed by the fellows—my own had come from my earnings delivering newspapers. But what was God saying to me about all this? Did He care about my riding bikes down center lines of busy boulevards or Brylcreem or Chippewa boots? Maybe He did if pleasing my peers became a problem for me as I set out onto my own ministry.

So that was my sermon: on testings. It lasted all of ten minutes and Mom had to do some quick thinking to fill in the unused time. The patient farmers were kind enough to compliment me on my preaching but I suspect they had to do a little confessing about stretching the truth that night when they got home. The main thing was that I'd spotted something through that experience which was, just possibly, going to be a real problem. What did "belonging" mean to me? What importance did I attach to people's opinions of me, especially if they were people I respected? Just possibly these other voices would be a real testing some day.

We were all about to be introduced to the tan-skinned girl who would change our lives.

Frankly, I wasn't paying much attention in church that morning just before my fifteenth birthday. I sat on the wooden theater seat in the auditorium of our church in West L.A. listening to Dad's sermon. But in fact my mind was miles away—at a certain used car lot. For months I had been saving up my paperboy money to buy a car. Not just any car—it had to be a '39 Chevy. I would paint it metallic blue. I'd strip the chrome off and lower the rear end like everyone else was doing.

Suddenly, something in the tone of my Dad's voice caught my attention. Dad was talking about an Arab child. He had just returned from his very first trip overseas—to the Holy Land—a gift from the men's Bible class. But it was Dad's voice that alerted me. His usual booming bass was softer—almost cracking.

"She was just a little ragged Arab girl, sticking her dusty hand out and pleading, *Baksheesh!* That's the Arabic word for alms. I'll never forget her face—not for the rest of my life. . . ."

Dad looked down at the wooden pulpit in front of him. He cleared his throat. The child, he said, had come up to him outside a Palestinian refugee camp. She was about eight. She wore a shabby dress, her hair was stringy and she carried a still younger girl on her hip.

"Our hosts told us not to give to beggars because it would encourage them, whatever that meant. But I just couldn't turn her away. I reached into my pocket and put some coins in her hand."

Dad stopped and I thought for a moment that he was going to cry. The church was very, very still. Dad went on to say that in his hotel room that same night he had knelt beside his bed. Suddenly the face of the dirty, tanned Palestinian child came before him. He shut his eyes, but she was still there. Again she reached out her hand, but as Dad looked into her pleading eyes, he said it seemed she wasn't begging *just* for a coin but for something far deeper. She was reaching out for comfort, encouragement, for love, hope for the future. The Gospel.

I looked down at my expensive Chippewa boots as Dad spoke. All our tears were freely flowing now. Dad told us how he lay awake all night in his hotel room, unable to forget the face of this girl. "And I have to tell you something," he said, pulling himself up straighter, "As of that night, I have changed. I want to give the rest of my life to telling people about the needs of our brothers and sisters overseas. I want to get involved in helping.

"World missions," Dad said, "used to be just a couple of words. But no more. From now on missions has a face. It is the face of a child."

My fifteen-year-old heart raced with a new excitement. Dad wasn't the only one who would never be the same. The words I had seen a year earlier, written in the air before me in my uncle's church in Arkansas, suddenly popped into my mind. "Go ye into all the world. . . ."

Maybe there was something I could give right now.

I tried not to think about my car.

Dad reversed his priorities at the church. More and more money was earmarked for overseas work. Amazingly, as the people turned their pockets inside out, the local bills were also paid—there was a thirty percent increase in our total church income.

Dad did things with a splash. For weeks he told us about the lives and challenges facing one particular African missionary until he had us all very interested.

Then one Sunday he had a brand new jeep driven right onto the platform of the church. It would go to help the African missionary if we could raise the money.

At last I had the focus I wanted. I committed myself to give the earning from my paper route for two months—$40—toward the purchase of the jeep. I didn't buy my souped-up Chevy, but I was helping to buy a vehicle which would go halfway around the world.

Later I got to wondering. Maybe I could still get my car. I persuaded Dad to let me take two extra jobs in addition to my paper route.

Sure enough, with great pride, which I must say my dad shared with me, I managed to save enough that summer of my fifteenth year to buy my first car. It was just what I wanted, too—a '39 Chevy. The poor automobile was already eleven years old and just barely staying alive. Both rear doors were broken. I stripped all the chrome off and with the help of a friend painted it metallic blue.

But something more subtle was stirring—a quiet, insistent voice inside told me that my life was to be more than cars or keeping up with others. A trip to Mexico over Easter vacation

25

with ten other fellows seemed to clinch it. I was eighteen, as most of the others were. We didn't know much about meeting people from another culture, but we used our high school Spanish to try to give the most important message on earth. Incredibly, about twenty Mexicans said yes, they did want to know Jesus. Some knelt right on the streets to pray. Even with the inglorious way our trip ended—two other guys and I were in the hospital with dysentery—I knew I had stumbled onto a signpost of guidance.

Something was germinating inside me that I didn't quite understand.

That trip to Mexico was probably the reason I decided that I wanted to go to the Assemblies' Bible college in Springfield, Missouri.

So one exciting day in the fall of 1954, when I was nineteen, my sister Phyllis and I (she had decided to go to Central Bible Institute, too) loaded all our things into my car, which by now had been upgraded to a '48 Dodge.

Mom and Dad and ten-year-old Jannie, wearing her saddleshoes, huddled on the sidewalk in front of our home in West L.A. waiting for us to finish loading up. Then the five of us gathered tightly together while Dad prayed for our physical and spiritual safety. There was a good deal of lip-biting as we pulled away from the curb.

But as I nosed my car east on Olympic Boulevard, heading for Springfield, 1500 miles away, I was about to be launched into an adventure that would take a lifetime to explore.

Chapter Four

Waves

It was just a trip to the Bahamas, but a unique experience of guidance there set the course of my life.

While in school in Missouri three other young men and I— we were all about twenty years old—decided to form a Gospel singing quartet. Over the holidays we took trips further from Springfield than we could reach on weekends. One of these took us to Nassau, the capital of the Bahama Islands.

It was June 1956, and we were aboard Mackey Airlines on the short hop from Miami to Nassau. Below our prop-driven plane lay a string of islands in the most improbably-colored water I had ever seen—broad bands of light aqua, deep turquoise and lavender.

When the missionary picked us up and drove down the left side of the road, I found myself intrigued as I had not been since I was eighteen and went with the ten others to Mexico. (It was hard to believe that was already two years ago!) The elation came from more than local color, the flowers, the traffic police with their white, tropical suits and pith helmets. It was something inside of *me*.

Between singing performances we talked with missionaries who were working in the Bahamas. They told us about an awkward situation on one of the out islands. Three teenagers had come down to do missionary work—totally on their own! They had started dating the island girls, not knowing that in the Bahamas dating was never casual, as it was in the States. And now the island was full of damaging rumors.

I listened with mixed emotions. I was sorry those teenagers had been insensitive. But in the back of my mind was a thought. "What a neat idea they had—young people coming here to do missionary work!"

IS THAT REALLY YOU, LORD?

That night after our singing engagement, I returned to the missionary's guest room with its white walls, unadorned except for an island scene in a cheap wooden frame. I lay down on the bed, doubled the pillow under my head and opened my Bible, routinely asking God to speak into my mind.

What happened next was far from routine.

Suddenly, I was looking at a map of the world. Only the map was alive, moving! I sat up. I shook my head, rubbed my eyes. It was a mental movie. I could see all the continents. Waves were crashing onto their shores. Each went onto a continent, then receded, then came up further until it covered the continent completely.

I caught my breath. Then, as I watched, the scene changed. The waves became young people—kids my age and even younger—covering the continents. They were talking to people on street corners and outside bars. They were going from house to house. They were preaching. Everywhere they were caring for people as Dad cared for the little girl reaching out for *baksheesh*.

Then the scene was gone.

Wow! I thought. *What was that?*

I looked where I had seen waves of young people but saw only the white wall of the guest room with the island print in its wooden frame. Had I imagined the vision or had God shown me the future?

Was that really you, Lord? I wondered, still staring at the wall, amazed. Young people—kids, really—going out as missionaries! What an idea! I thought about the three boys on the out islands and the harm they had done by just being normal kids. If this strange picture really had come from God, there must be a way to avoid problems yet harness youthful energies.

Why, I thought, *did God give me this vision? Was my future somehow linked to the waves of young people?* For a long time I lay there, staring at nothing at all.

One thing was certain. I should tell no one about the vision. Not until I understood what it meant.

There seemed to be a pattern emerging: God would speak

giving a distinct call, then a testing would come. When I was a young teenager, God spoke giving the call of *baksheesh;* the question was whether I'd try to keep up with the guys with my Chippewa boots and '39 Chevy or hear that call. Now, two days after the strange vision of the waves, came the early stage of a bigger testing. What a paradox that it came as the result of a good turn of events, one which would put me in touch with my family's past.

When we got to Miami for our next engagement and checked into a motel, the others wanted me to go out. "Loren, we're ready to go eat. You coming?"

"No, thanks, I think I'll pass."

There was something on my mind. This was Miami and a broken family tie was here that was more important to me right then than a meal. I knew my Aunt Arnette lived here—the one who disowned Dad 27 years ago when he decided to become a preacher. Other relatives told us Aunt Arnette had done well for herself; she owned a furniture factory and several retail stores in the area. As for the youngest sister, Aunt Sandra, no one seemed to know where she was. Aunt Arnette was still bitter. Dad managed to get through to her three years ago when Granddad Cunningham died. "I wouldn't cross the street to come to his funeral," said my aunt.

What would happen if I tried to call her? I thought to myself.

As soon as I was alone, I reached into the drawer beside the bed and pulled out the phone book. A shiver of excitement swept over me. There it was—the same name in the phone book. Arnette Cunningham. Could it be my Aunt Arnette? I dialed.

"Hello?"

Her voice! I had never heard it before, of course, yet it had a familiar timbre—she *sounded* like a Cunningham.

"Hello, I'm Loren Cunningham. My father is Thomas Cecil Cunningham. I wonder if I'm your nephew and if I could meet you?"

A silence. Then, "No, I can't! I'm too busy!" Click.

The next day was Saturday. My friends were going swimming and as much as I loved beaches I surprised myself by choosing again to stay back. Alone in the motel room, I stretched out on the bed and looked at the phone. I couldn't forget that conversation. It had opened a whole closetful of family memories.

I leaned against the headboard of the bed, staring across the little motel room. Our unopened letters had been sent back, phone calls refused. Yet something about the sound of that strange but familiar voice made me want to try once more. I reached for the phone.

"Hello, this is Loren again. I'm sorry to bother you, but tomorrow I'll be leaving town. I wonder if I could meet you?"

"I'm sorry but my employees are having a birthday party for me today and I couldn't possibly see you."

Aunt Arnette hung up again but I'd made an inch of progress. At least she gave an *excuse* for not seeing me. I got an idea and went shopping.

What do you buy for a woman's birthday when you don't know her? I decided on a linen handkerchief with lots of lace, like Mom always loved. Then I carefully chose a birthday card—not too sentimental, but one that said "Happy Birthday Aunt."

By Sunday noon we were ready to leave town. I called from a phone booth on Biscayne Boulevard, asking her for just a few minutes of her time before I left town. This time Aunt Arnette, perhaps out of sheer curiosity, agreed to see me.

We drove our station wagon through palm-fringed streets where houses sat comfortably amidst tropical landscaping. We pulled up before a large grey-blue house with a screened front porch. Remembering Arnette's words, scorning my dad for choosing to "tramp through life, living off of charity with religion as an excuse," I hastily checked my hair in the rearview mirror and straightened my tie.

As I got out, leaving the others to wait in the car, I could see the shadowy outline of a lady watching me from the screened porch. I walked measuredly up to the steps.

Then I was face to face with a woman who looked like Dad. She had carefully-coifed hair and diamonds on her fingers but strangely, somehow, there was a sense of belonging.

"Hi, I'm Tom's boy."

Aunt Arnette looked me over slowly, searching my features. There was a long silence as we stood there on the steps.

"I bought you this for your birthday," I said at last, handing her the card with the handkerchief tucked inside.

Aunt Arnette took the card. "You look so much like your father!" she said. And then, softly, ". . . the same brown hair, the same eyes. The same smile. But you're a little taller, aren't you?" There was a heartbeat's pause. She smiled, wavering, then suddenly her eyes filled. "It's been so long. . . ."

Then she was urging me to come inside and to bring my friends, too. But no, I said as I stepped in, we really did have only a few minutes. I answered her quick questions about my parents, explaining that I, too, was preparing to be a minister, going to school in Missouri and traveling with the singing group through the summer. We had just come from the Bahamas. She asked how far north we would be going. I told her and there was another silence as her eyes continued to measure me. Then she said carefully, "You have another aunt you know, Loren. Compared to your Aunt Sandra, I'm a pauper."

That was quite a statement, I thought, glancing around me. When Aunt Arnette learned that our tour would take us near Aunt Sandra's summer home, she urged me to contact her.

I looked at my watch. It really was time to go. We shook hands and she asked how she could find me. I left her a copy of our itinerary.

A few days later Aunt Arnette called us on our tour to say she'd arranged for me to meet Sandra. A chauffeur was sent to the Pentecostal church where we were singing to drive me to Aunt Sandra's summer home in Lake Placid, New York. Aunt Sandra and her husband, George, moved in a glamorous world I had never known before. But what really impressed me was Aunt Sandra herself. It was hard to believe she was 50, with her laughing gray eyes and wavy, short brown hair. She was kind, too, making me feel totally at ease—reminding me of my sister Phyllis. Aunt Sandra took me in like a long-lost son. Even Uncle George, a tall, cool New Englander, was cordial.

The extent of their acceptance of me was demonstrated before my last year at Central Bible Institute. My parents and I had worried about how we were going to come up with my tuition. But Aunt Sandra wrote to say that they had decided to provide the money for me to continue my education—as far as I cared to go.

The next year Dad, Arnette and Sandra were reunited. A happy ending, I smiled to myself. What I didn't see at all was that the reunion had set the stage for a major testing.

Chapter Five

Small Beginnings

"Well, son, you're certainly moving fast!" Mom said one day as I searched my closet for a dress shirt. I was 24, and in the three years since returning to California from college it had been convenient to move back with the folks who were living in a hillside house in Monterey Park.

"Yes," I said absently. I wasn't sure that Mom meant her comment as a compliment, but I was glad she had noticed.

"But son, you need to keep everything on the altar. If you get proud, God can't use you."

After Mom left the room I walked over to the window, looking at the cactus plants outside. My thoughts raced over the last year at school where I was valedictorian and president of the student body; and to my ordination as an Assemblies of God minister; and to the good job I had now as leader of youth activities in the Los Angeles area. I was glad for all that but . . . proud? Mom usually hit the mark with blunt accuracy but this time I felt she had missed it. It would be years before I saw the truth in her words.

Right now I was far more concerned with my restlessness. What was missing? I enjoyed my work—the young people were all so bright and eager. But I had to admit that most of the activities I planned for them were empty. They missed the heart of the young people because they had no challenge. That's what we all long for, especially in our teens and early twenties. The big challenge.

I remembered again that strange vision I had seen in the Bahamas . . . was it already four years ago? The contrast between that vision and my little efforts was cruel. It was time to do something.

So a few days later, I went to my district leader with the idea of taking teens on a missionary trip to Hawaii. The plan was approved and we did go. With 106 people! We had mixed results though—half of them only wanted to be on the beaches, the other half wanted to talk to people about their faith. *You can't mix purposes, Loren,* I said to myself.

Odd! I found that I was tucking away certain experiences, making a mental list. One: from the three boys in the Bahamas (who caused such a stir dating local girls) I saw that once on a mission, dating was out. Two: from Hawaii I learned that you can't mix sightseeing with the single-minded purpose of evangelism.

Why was I making notes to myself like this? And why I was returning so often to that vision of the waves which I had seen in the Bahamas? The unusual memory just wouldn't go away. It seemed to spoil me for the ordinary activities of life.

I had to find out what that experience meant and what God wanted me to do with it. Maybe the best way would be to go out by myself for a while to scout out the possibilities overseas. My travel agent got me a super-discounted, around-the-world ticket. To raise the money I sold my car, took a leave of absence from my job as youth director and set out to see a world that was in trouble. I knew I was not sightseeing. Enjoying new experiences, yes— but with a strange certainty that I was being guided toward something I could not yet see.

As I traveled, what hit me the hardest was that people are people everywhere. We are just enclosed by "systems" that separate us. In India the fact that millions had utterly different beliefs from my own took on a gut reality in an experience that took place in an isolated village.

It was a dark, hot night and I was returning to my hotel room when I heard an unearthly wail coming from a crowd and decided to investigate. Making my way to the middle of the commotion I saw a huge pile of sticks. A man with a torch put the sticks afire and by the growing light I saw on top of the pyre some thin legs and a still-boyish frame. I learned from someone who spoke English that the sixteen-year-old boy had been killed in a knife fight. The wailing reached a feverish pitch and I stood there with the people in the firelight, overcome with the realization that this boy had gone out into the void. There was heavy, unrelieved despair hanging in the air, mixed with the sickish, sweet smell of burning flesh.

I couldn't forget the hopelessness in that group around the pyre. I was left with an overwhelming wish. I wanted to be able to say to those who were still alive: There is hope and His name is Jesus.

Another thing was happening to me on that trip. Something far more personal.

I began to feel terribly alone, incomplete. I had dated a lot of girls during my college days in Springfield and through my days working on my Master's at the University of Southern California. But these friendships, even some quite serious friendships, just never led anywhere.

And now, suddenly, I felt that I was missing an essential part of life. Why was I out here all alone scouting? It hit me hardest when I visited the magnificent Taj Mahal. As I walked through the ornate keyhole arches, I gasped. There, reflected perfectly in the huge rectangular pool, gleaming in the white hot Indian sun, stood the alabaster monument. And all of it was done by a man for the love of a woman.

I felt so alone as I walked through the archway. I wanted to say to someone, "Isn't that beautiful!" But no one was there.

What am I doing here, all alone? I thought again as I walked beside the giant reflecting pool, seeing my lone image looking back. *Why don't I have someone to share with—not only beauty, like the Taj Mahal, but dreams too, of being able to bring hope?* I thought of parents wailing as their own youngster was sent into a void. And I thought of the beggars' hands reaching out to me everywhere. Just as Dad had done, I'd dug into my pocket and put coins into as many hands as possible, but there were always more hands still empty. It was overwhelming. Somehow I wanted to say to a partner, "There must be a way to help these people, to meet their heart needs and their physical needs too."

But where would I find a girl who'd understand that as well as the vision of the waves of young people going out as missionaries? Who would tramp around with me trying to find out if the vision really came from the Lord? She'd certainly need to have, (as Mom would put it) a "calling" of her own. And, thinking about

35

Mom, who would be bold enough to fit in with my family, all so individualistic and spicy and strong? Especially Mom, I smiled to myself!

Finally, I returned to the folks' home in California. I began (alone again, and aware of it) to travel around the country describing what I had experienced. I was especially interested in telling young people about the primitive, not-so-clean-and-comfortable world that was out there, teeming with opportunities to do something important. When it came to telling them just *what* they could do, though, I was a little vague because it still wasn't clear to me.

I met Dallas and Larry a month after I got back from my trip while speaking at their church in Bakersfield, California.

Dallas Moore, 21, had a square-jawed face, with twinkling blue eyes, brown crewcut and the build of a football player. He and a friend, Larry Hendricks, also 21, took me out for a sandwich at Stan's Restaurant. Both boys, I learned, were heavy equipment operators, running bulldozers, backhoes and cranes.

But as we drove toward Stan's Restaurant the subject was not heavy equipment. It was cars. Dallas' own car was one you noticed—a '56 two-toned aqua and white Bel Aire Chevrolet, squeaky clean (there was not a fingerprint on the chrome) with white tuck-and-roll upholstery. I was remembering my '39 Chevy and I realized how important my car had seemed to me ten years ago.

But something was wrong. As they talked about twin cams, dual manifolds and triple carburetors, I just wasn't *with* the conversation. We slid into a booth at Stan's and the waitress brought our water and left. I lifted my glass. Cold. Clean. No fear of bacteria here. I looked around me at the other cozy booths, filled with people happily devouring mounds of hamburgers and french fries. Dallas and Larry did not notice my sudden silence. Everyone in the place seemed to be enclosed in a giant isolation bubble—laughing, having a good time while outside were those crowds with outstretched beggars' hands.

It was too much. Abruptly I changed the conversation. I

began to tell Dallas and Larry about my trip. It all spilled out. The beggars. The sixteen-year-old burning on the funeral pyre. The hopelessness, the wailing. I looked at Dallas and Larry and there was a glint in their eyes—they were seeing it all through me.

"And the really great thing is, guys, there's so much you can do to make a difference out there!" I said.

They were agreeing with me, but then came the inevitable question. "Yeah, Loren, we would like to help. But how could we? We aren't missionaries. We drive bulldozers."

Yes, that was the question. How?

A month after talking to Dallas and Larry, I was driving down Pacific Coast Highway towards L.A. with some friends, Bob and Lorraine Theetge. Bob, a tall, still-boyish 40-year-old, was a businessman. He and his pert, black-eyed wife were part of a church where I had worked in Inglewood.

As we hummed down the highway, with the waves crashing onto the beach just feet away, I began to think of my dilemma.

Everywhere, I had been meeting kids like Dallas and Larry and they were ready . . . *eager* . . . to do something important. One young man had written on a card, "I'm ready to die for Jesus!" I held that card in my hand and suddenly saw the wrong I had been doing. I had been telling young people to give their lives away yet the present system required years of schooling first, by which time most would have forgotten their fiery zeal. I was all for education and was working on my Master's at USC, but I'd had strong motivations that propelled me through school without losing sight of my calling.

I knew I could no longer challenge young people when there was no channel for them.

I looked out the car window at the surf rolling in and remembered the vision. It was time to do something, but what?

"Loren, you're a million miles away!" Lorraine said, grinning at me from the front seat.

"At least a few thousand miles," I admitted. "I've been thinking . . . about kids, and how they want to do something that really counts." I began to tell Bob and Lorraine about the shocking needs in the world and what I saw as the wasted resources of youthful energy. As I spoke I found myself referring to the mental notes I'd been making. We should recruit young people, send them out immediately—right after high school, so that later even going to college would have a new and deeper purpose. We'd send them for short periods of missionary service—a couple of months or a year. Everyone would know he was there for work, not sightseeing. Each would pay his own way. (No one would be along for a free ride to see the world.) One more thing sprang out, big in my mind. It was new, but it had that ring of certainty: whatever missionary work we did, we should be open to volunteers from all churches not just one denomination. I was astonished to see how clear my thinking had become.

And then Bob said three little words.

He turned slightly toward me and said quietly, "Let's do it!"

I knew in that instant that something had begun. Bob didn't say, *"You* do it," he said, *"Let's* do it!"

Sometimes God speaks spectacularly, I thought to myself, as with the vision of the waves in the Bahamas. But just now, He had spoken through three words from a friend. "Let's do it!"

We decided on a name and started Youth With A Mission in December of 1960. We set about looking for our first volunteers. Needing some place to meet with recruits, I turned my bedroom at the folks' house into an office. "I can help you get a naugahyde sofabed, Loren," suggested Lorraine. "That'll give you room for a desk."

Soon Bob and I were lugging a brown sofabed into my bedroom-turned-office. With one typewriter and a used mimeograph machine which we set up in my folks' garage we began printing our first announcements which we planned to send to a list of pastors for distribution to their young people.

I enlisted Mom, Dad and Jannie, now a high schooler, to help fold, address and stamp the 180 just-dried announcements. We worked on the living room floor by the big windows looking out over the San Gabriel Valley. My sister Phyllis escaped the chore because she now had a home of her own, having married Navy Lieutenant Leonard Griswold. They were both teaching school in Los Angeles and Phyllis was expecting their first child in January.

"Hey, big brother, how come I'm not getting paid for this?" said Jannie.

"You'll get your reward in heaven, sis!" I laughed. But I thought again about the conditions we were laying out in the papers we were folding. Service without pay—in fact, paying their own way to go! Rugged evangelism, not sightseeing. And no dating.

When I carefully placed the bundles of newsletters in front of our local postmaster, I imagined the response we'd get back from everyone. "Where *has* this idea been?" they'd all say. "This is great!"

The reaction wasn't long in coming, but it was hardly what I had expected. Oh, the kids were excited. Already we were getting letters back from potential volunteers. It was Dad who alerted me to the fact that some leaders were less than enthusiastic. (By now, Dad was no longer pastoring a church for he had been elected as a local official in our denomination—with a special portfolio for missions.) I decided to go to Springfield and speak to those in charge of missions.

They were cordial enough to me, a young greenhorn, but they pointed out all the problems in my plan. Inexperienced young people would be an explosive element overseas, they explained. With rising nationalism and political unrest, the denomination had its hands full keeping the *experienced* missionaries from getting kicked out. And there were the complexities of different cultures. And, there were real dangers and diseases. The last thing they needed was a bunch of thrill-seeking kids complicating the worthwhile job the real missionaries were trying to do.

One of the men must have seen me wilting, because he leaned forward and made a counter-proposal.

"Now, if you were to send out *vocational volunteers*, Loren—say to some really well-established compounds where they could be properly supervised," he paused letting this idea sink in, "why if you were to do that, I'd stand on a chair and cheer you on!"

Why not? I thought.

As soon as I returned to California, I learned about a great opportunity in Liberia for some heavy equipment operators to

build a road through the jungle to a leper colony. I immediately
thought of Dallas Moore and Larry Hendricks. I called Dallas in
Bakersfield and explained how he and Larry could be our very
first volunteers. When he asked about money, I explained that
they'd be responsible for their own funding. Dallas said he'd talk
to his folks and to Larry, and I waited several anxious days. Finally
he called me back. I held my breath while he began in his slow way
to tell how they had talked it over with their pastors and their
folks, and . . . well . . . they felt it was right.

Great, I shouted inside! It's actually starting!

Then Dallas added one more thing. "And as for the money
Loren, well, I'm selling my Chevy."

Lorraine Theetge continued to work every day without salary, as were all of us. (My own income came from occasional
offerings given to me at speaking dates.) By now we had a
nickname among ourselves for Youth With A Mission—we called
it Y–WAM (rhymes with "I am"), and the volunteers were
"Y–WAM–ers."

Before Dallas and Larry finished their preparations for leaving for the leper colony in Liberia, we had several more
YWAMers getting ready to go to other mission posts.

I was so busy scouting out possibilities for new recruits that I
was in Nigeria when Dallas and Larry headed off for their year in
Liberia that October. Dad told me in a letter that they had a great
send-off; Dad and others had clustered around the two boys in
the L.A. airport, laid their hands on them and prayed for them.
Then Dallas and Larry boarded the 707 TWA jet for Liberia.

Fantastic! I thought, re-folding the letter. The first two
YWAMers were on their way. It wasn't waves yet, but it was a
beginning. I just knew that thousands more would soon be going
out like Dallas and Larry.

Back in the United States, I made plans to spend a day with
Aunt Sandra. She and Uncle George had asked me to visit them.
She said there was something they wanted to talk to me about. I
was sure it was a job—a very *good* job. I called Aunt Sandra and
told her I could come by during my trip.

And so it was that I had found myself once more welcomed into the comfortable world of George and Sandra Meehan.

I twisted in the silk sheets, and peered out at the sky. I had not fallen asleep until very late and now the sun was high, bathing the elegant bedroom in whiteness. Today Aunt Sandra was no doubt going to offer me that job and I'd have to tell her I'd heard the voice of God telling me to take another path. It was going to be difficult. The question was, would I continue to obey? I traced my finger over the monogram on Aunt Sandra's silk sheets. I certainly did enjoy the nicer things. Ever since I'd worked so hard on my paper route to get myself some Chippewa boots and a Chevy with metallic blue paint, I had had an appreciation for quality *things*. It was a good feeling being here in these surroundings, riding in Aunt Sandra's Cadillac—even driving it occasionally.

I looked at my watch. Nine o'clock! I rang for Hawkins who appeared in minutes bearing a breakfast tray with all my favorites—ripe melon, waffles, eggs, bacon and a tall glass of fresh-squeezed orange juice.

I hurriedly ate and went downstairs. Uncle George had left already, but I went through the French doors in the back of the house to find my aunt waiting for me on the terrace. She stood and greeted me with a cool kiss on my cheek. Gail, the boxer, was circling my legs, licking my hands.

"Loren! Good morning, dear! How did you sleep?"

"Fine," I said half-heartedly, "just a little long, I'm afraid!" We went over to the lawn furniture and sat down.

"Loren, we're so glad you were able to come by. I've . . . we've been anxious to know if you would consider coming to work with Uncle George."

Here it was! The question I knew I had to answer, the moment I had come here to face. I really cared for this lady and I understood all too well the generosity of Uncle George's invitation. What they were offering was a chance to become part of their multimillion dollar family business—like a son, an heir. It was ironic that I was facing the same temptation my Dad had

41

faced, so many years before when Sandra and Arnette had generously tried to help him with his education. Now, here I was a generation later with the same test from one of the same sisters. And the fact that I cared so much for her made it all the harder to do what I knew I had to do.

"Let's go for a walk," I said, stalling.

Gail jumped up and ran ahead of us as we strolled across the expanse of lawn toward the sea wall and Lake Worth that lapped at the back of their property.

We stood together, looking across the broad body of water. I took a deep breath.

"It isn't that I don't marvel at what you've offered me, Aunt Sandra—"

"But you're saying *no*, is that it?"

I tried to describe—not explain, for I couldn't—how I had heard that call to preach when I was thirteen. And how again when I was twenty God had showed me with that vision of waves of young people taking His good news to every continent of the world. Somehow, as I heard my voice telling her about my vision, it sounded presumptuous.

"I've heard all this, Loren," said Aunt Sandra, her voice soft but a little edgy. "But at least, couldn't you just do your work in the United States? There are plenty of people right here who need help." (And think of all the help you could give them if you had thousands of dollars at your disposal, a voice inside said.)

I looked at Aunt Sandra's face and saw the worry and concern and a knife twisted inside me. I hated letting her down, but I knew I had to put this test behind. I found my voice.

"I can't, Aunt Sandra. I just cannot. It's to the whole world that God has called me and I have to obey."

Aunt Sandra turned and took both of my hands. "Loren, Loren. Our family has been torn apart too much already by religion. Let's not have it happen again. Good luck in your work. And give my love to your Mom and Dad. I'll explain to Uncle George. As best I can, I'll explain."

It was over. I walked through the big double doors and down the wide marble stairs, hearing Hawkins closing them firmly behind me. I turned once and caught a glimpse of Aunt Sandra at the library window.

I determined as my taxi drove me away from the Meehan home that I was going to stay close to Aunt Sandra and Aunt Arnette, but no matter what, I would stay true to my calling. As we drove over the bridge toward the airport, I wondered about my next step and the waves. Waves? We now had six volunteers out or on their way. Hardly waves. Merely a trickle.

Chapter Six

Helpmate, Wife and Friend

How could I have ever guessed that the young lady in the frumpy dress would be so important to me?

It was two years since we'd started YWAM and I was riding with some new friends, Ed and Enid Scratch and their daughter, Darlene, to a lunch date in the San Francisco Bay area. The blond girl (I guessed she was in her early twenties) sat on the far side of the back seat. She was almost hostile-quiet, and dressed in such a drab dress—some black and brown checked thing. I had met lots of girls in my 27 years and I figured this one must be very conservative. Again and again, though, I found my eyes wandering over to Darlene. She would never look at me, but she wouldn't initiate conversation with her parents either, as if some small tension lay between. She did have pretty, honey-colored hair and she certainly filled out that nondescript outfit nicely.

"They have a great smorgasbord at this place, Loren," Darlene's father said, filling an awkward silence as we drove up to Dinah's Shack. And he was right. We all made our way down the long serving tables groaning under a delicious array. We settled into our food with short bits of conversation interrupting long stretches of silence.

"What is this Youth With A Mission?" Darlene asked abruptly, her blue eyes looking straight at me.

"Uh, well, I . . . that is we . . . want to see waves of young people going out as missionaries." I didn't have a lot more to report, actually. Dad had recently visited Dallas and Larry in Liberia. They were doing great, building their jungle road to the leper colony as well as going to remote villages, telling people about the great God who made us all. I explained to Darlene the vocational volunteer program, the opportunities for kids to help the regular missionaries with their skills. To my surprise Darlene suddenly became more attentive.

44

"How many volunteers have you sent out so far?"

"Ten."

When I said it, I found I'd dropped my voice. The number sounded pitifully small. I was still working out of my suitcase. But I did have a staff of two now! Lorraine Theetge had an elderly lady named Mrs. Overton helping her. Two staffers and a handful of volunteers. Not very impressive.

"Well I think it's a great idea, don't you, dear?" Darlene's mother asked her husband, rescuing me.

Darlene's father agreed a bit too enthusiastically, then went to pay the bill. The four of us drove back to Ed Scratch's church where only my olive VW bug and one other car were left in the parking lot. The other vehicle was a black '39 Ford hot-rod with a lowered front. "Whose car is that?" I asked Darlene, pointing out the window of her father's car.

"It's mine'" Darlene said. "It's not a Thunder*bird*—so I call it Thunder*goose!*"

Hmmm. This girl was not as mousey as I thought. I got out of her parents' car and went around to open the rear door. I noticed, as I did so, that Darlene grabbed a quick glance in the rearview mirror and fluffed her hair with her fingers. Getting out, she accidentally brushed against me and I didn't mind a bit.

Darlene seemed in no hurry to leave after her parents drove away. We leaned against her rakish black Ford and talked into the afternoon. It was one of those perfect California days with a light breeze coming in from the Pacific. I learned that Darlene had a fulfilling job as a registered nurse. Darlene herself came from a long line of preachers and missionaries in the Assemblies of God. When I said that I hoped to see a thousand young people in the mission field, however, Darlene became silent.

"You don't think *all* Christians have a call, do you, Loren?" she asked at last. "Everybody can't be a preacher."

"Everybody can't be a preacher, but every Christian does have a call of his own." I paused. Something prompted me to add, "or *her* own, Darlene. You have to obey that call—no matter who tries to get you off the track."

There was another silence. Somewhere down the street I could hear kids shouting in a neighborhood ballgame. I was afraid I had offended this girl and surprisingly I hoped that I had not

45

done so. Finally she spoke. And with a grin. "You're absolutely right, Cunningham!"

I liked her. No coyness, no cat-and-mouse games. Why was I suddenly remembering the Taj Mahal?

I was glad to be back in Southern California in time to meet Dallas and Larry as they flew in from their year in Liberia. I got their story as we drove. Dallas' square face shone with excitement as he told me about building the road through the jungle, and about their weekend evangelistic work. The adventure, he said, was the most important thing that had happened in his life. I said goodbye, knowing that no matter what Dallas and Larry did after this, they would carry with them an extra dimension—a knowledge that they had played a vital part in taking the Gospel to all the world.

But even as we rounded off this experience with our first volunteers I was aware of the incredible size of the task ahead of us.

As I drove home, I remembered an unsettling experience I had had on my early scouting trip to Africa before sending out Dallas and Larry. I'd visited a village where I was the very first person to bring the message of Jesus. The old chief had nodded his assent when I told him through an interpreter that God had given His Son for the world. I watched as the chief and others weighed their decisions.

A few weeks later, I boarded a plane to leave the Congo. I looked out the porthole and saw a thin column of smoke—an evening fire coming from a village just like the one I had visited. Then I saw two, three more. Everywhere, on the horizon, the smoke of village fires was ascending. The enormity of what Jesus had told us to do—go into *all* the world and preach the gospel to every creature—hit me as it was graphically portrayed below my plane, etched by hundreds of village fires in the sky's twilight.

Dallas and Larry were back in Bakersfield. I was on the road again and I still found myself remembering the girl in the dull dress. I called Darlene and found her friendly enough but I sensed she was still holding back. Later, I called again and wrote her but we could never seem to find a way to get together. Finally I decided on a different tack. I learned that Darlene had canceled a plan to come to L.A. to see her aunt.

"Darlene," I said on the phone, "I want to see you. PSA has a flight leaving San Francisco this Friday at eight o'clock. I will be waiting for you at the L.A. airport. If you're not on board, I will fly to where you are."

Which is how we came to have our first proper date, a few days later. Darlene was lovely in a yellow suit, with every blond hair in place. Her manner, though, was still reserved. I was off balance, enjoying her company but wondering what she was keeping from me.

On our fourth date, I drove Darlene in my VW bug up to a summit which afforded a panoramic view of Los Angeles. The lights of the city glittered like jewels in black velvet. Darlene was primly trying to hug the far side of my bug.

"Dar," I began, using her nickname, "is there something you need to tell me?"

She looked at me directly, and said, "You're a good friend, Loren. You really are. . . ."

"You're about to say 'but.' But *what?*"

"Loren, you were really right when you told me that I shouldn't let *anyone* stand in the way of obeying God. There was someone—" (my heart perked at the little word *was*) "his name was Joe."

Slowly, the story unfolded as Dar stared at the gleaming city lights. She told me that when she was nine years old she had a vision of herself surrounded by Asian children. Her heart told her it was a call: she was to be a missionary. But fourteen years had passed and she had fallen in love with Joe, who was not at all interested in missions. Unknown to her parents, Dar was considering marrying Joe, pushing her call to the back of her mind.

"My folks felt something was wrong and were worried. That's why Dad twisted my arm into going with them to Dinah's Shack that day—they were hoping I'd meet someone to get my mind off Joe. I was so mad I decided to do the minimum—just be polite. And I wore my ugliest dress!"

I chuckled, but she smiled and went on. My comment about obeying God's call convinced her that she had to stop fooling herself. The same night, she got down on her knees and gave up Joe.

"I told God I'd obey Him whatever the cost! I'd be an old-maid missionary if He wanted." I started to interrupt her, but she continued. "I asked God to take away my love for Joe." The next day an amazing thing happened. Joe called her demanding to know what happened at 10:30 the night before. He said at that time he suddenly knew he had lost her.

"But Dar," I said, when she stopped talking, "there's one thing wrong. Did God actually tell you to be an old-maid mission-ary or did you add that part?"

Her silence told me I had hit the mark. She had thought that, for her, serving God as a missionary would preclude marriage. Now I knew why she had been friendly but had kept the careful distance.

There was one more thing I had to find out about this girl. I knew now that she and I both had a call to missions. And her spunk and cheerfulness told me she might even handle living out of a suitcase with me. But could she mesh gears with my family? With Mom?

At our next meeting I drove Dar to my folks' home—the same one where my bedroom had become our first YWAM office two years before. As we walked past the cactus and yucca plants to the front door, I found myself wondering how it would go. Would Dar see that Mom's bark was worse than her bite? Would Mom like her?

Mom and Dad met us at the door, Dad's large square frame filling the doorway, Mom standing tall, her black eyes frankly looking Dar over from head to toe. "Hello there, young lady!" Dad boomed, offering his big hand. Mom didn't say a thing. I held my breath.

And then . . . the worst of all possible things happened.

Mom began to feel Dar's shoulders and arms, then she blurted, "You're too bony . . . and your skirt's too short!"

"I am not and it is not," Darlene responded instantly, not missing a beat. She said it with a grin, too! "How do you do, Mrs. Cunningham?" Darlene was offering her hand, her blue eyes twinkling. A second stretched out as Mom stood there, cocking her head. Then she threw up her hands, let out a big laugh and enveloped Dar in a hug. I let my breath out. I had found a girl who could stand up to Mom—and love her too!

Over the next few weeks Dar and I kept PSA Airlines busy between San Francisco and L.A. Before Christmas, only four months after we met, Darlene and I were in Blum's Restaurant in San Francisco, sitting on white wrought iron chairs, enjoying a crunch cake.

"Darlene, I'd like to spend the rest of my life with you." She mumbled something and changed the subject. Later I tried again. "I'm serious, Dar. I am asking you to marry me!"

This time she said, "I'll have to think about it'" Then quickly, "I've thought about it. Yes!"

I gathered her into my arms and kissed her. God had given me my partner and my heart soared with joy!

Three weeks later, on her birthday, January 5, 1963, I gave her a diamond ring and we set the wedding date for June 14—a little over six months away. In the excitement of making plans for a lifetime together, neither Dar nor I knew how soon we would face a major issue and an important aspect of guidance. We'd need to hear clearly from God about the unique ministry He had planned for each of us.

Chapter Seven

God Will Speak to You Directly

I squeezed in a trip to the Bahamas during Easter, just two months before our wedding day. It would be good to see those turquoise-striped waters again after seven years, but my purpose was to scout out possible locations for something really big. For the first time since our mixed-results experiment of taking teenagers to Hawaii three years ago, I wanted to take out another group, a hundred or more, to put into practice what I had seen in the waves. By now, we had recruited twenty vocational volunteers, but I longed for something more dynamic—closer to what I'd seen in the vision.

The flower-lined streets of Nassau hadn't changed, nor had the policemen in the white uniforms and pith helmets. As we drove by a beautiful beach, I recalled seeing the continents, the powerful surf covering them, the kids preaching, helping people.

Wouldn't it be just like the Lord to let us have our first big wave right here where He gave me the vision! I thought. I'd long ago noticed that God often gives advance hints of His plans. If we had a hundred kids, I thought, we could possibly reach every home on every one of the thirty out islands of the Bahamas.

The next morning I visited with local leaders from several churches including my host's church, Evangelistic Temple, a low concrete block building in Nassau, and explained our dream of having a hundred young people come here the following summer. The kids, I said, would pay their own way. They'd be here to work, not play; they'd give their entire summer to the evangelistic project. The name would say it all: Summer of Service. We'd give ourselves in service to Jesus.

The response was exactly what I'd hoped for, a hearty invitation. I was excited as I left the church that morning. When I got back home in a few days, I'd be able to tell Dar that we already had our first major YWAM project.

I hurried back to California to my fiancee. We had a classic June wedding in Dar's folks' church. She came down the aisle to me, wearing a white silk gown, her blue eyes sparkling under the veil. My Dad and Dar's father shared the ceremony, leading us in our vows. My sister Phyllis sang a solo and her husband, Len, was one of my groomsmen. Jannie lit the candles while Mom beamed from her front row seat.

Two very special guests were Aunt Arnette and Aunt Sandra. They sat on opposite ends of the serving table at the wedding reception, pouring tea and coffee from silver pitchers. I had a feeling of completion, of a broken circle mended.

"Here, Loren darling," Aunt Sandra said, putting down her coffee pitcher and ladling me some fruit punch. "You have a lovely bride, dear, and I know she'll help you with your work." Aunt Sandra returned to pouring coffee, but I knew that it was all right now—Aunt Sandra was rooting for me *and* my calling, no longer trying to pull me away from it.

In front of the Taj Mahal, I had asked God for a partner—I saw it now as a prayer, though at the time it had been only an unspoken yearning. I was looking for a girl who herself had a call to missions, who could mesh with my crazy lifestyle and with my family. Dar fit the bill in every way. There was one more thing I was anxious to discover—how she could find her own role in that calling.

We decided to take a missions trip through Europe and Asia—right after our honeymoon—to see if Dar would hear from God what her role was to be. We grabbed a honeymoon weekend in Carmel, California, then stored our wedding gifts in the folks' house. Before leaving for overseas, I took Dar by to see our "nest egg"—a four-bedroom house in La Puente. I'd been able to buy it with a small down payment, finance the rest with Dad as a co-signer, and rent it out to cover the payments. "It'll be a little security for the future," I pointed out to my bride.

51

Our upcoming Summer of Service in the Bahamas was only a year away, but for now our priority was each other and finding out how to work as a team. After all, I had been at this for three years now, and this was Dar's first introduction. The last thing I wanted her to feel like was a tag-along.

Our trip was half over as we stood together before the Taj Mahal. We arrived at a full moon. We stood with our arms around each other, gazing at this huge pearl-like structure, gleaming in the blue light. I could really understand as I looked down at Dar, her hair catching the moonlight, why a man would build such an extravagant monument to his wife.

I thought everything was going so well that what happened next took me by surprise. We were in Singapore, living in the small guest room of a mission house built in the days when the British controlled the island. The house had thick walls, high ceilings, creaky fans, bare wooden floors and square windows with bars.

One day I came in to find Dar thrown across the bed. I hurried across the dark wooden floor to her side.

"Dar! Are you sick?" I turned her to me and saw that her eyes were swollen and red from crying. "What's wrong?"

Dar did not answer right away. The old ceiling fan futilely pushed around the hot, humid air. "Nothing," she said. "Nothing really, honey."

Why do women say that, I wondered. "Of course it's something, Dar. Tell me."

A fly buzzed in wide circles above the four-postered bed. In the distance, I could hear a Moslem priest calling the faithful to prayer. But, bit by bit, the story fell out. "Honey," Dar said, "I . . . they all want me to be somebody I'm not." In country after country it seemed, friends had welcomed my new bride and innocently asked her, "Do you play the piano?" "No," Dar had to say. "Do you sing?" "No." "Which Bible school did you go to?" "Saint Francis School of Nursing." "Oh."

"Loren," Dar said, sitting up and dabbing her eyes, "I've been praying that God would do something to my voice—you know how I sound—so that I could sing."

I laughed and assured her that if I had have wanted a girl who

52

could sing and play the piano, I would've married one. "Dar," I said, "it sounds as if you want me to tell you what your role is." I held her hand but I was remembering something that kept me from trying to bolster her right now. I recalled myself as a little boy praying desperately behind the couch for my dying daddy, and a man who came to the door with a "vision" about Dad coming home in a coffin, and then Mom's voice saying, "With something this important, God will have to tell *me*."

I pulled Dar close and steeled myself. Then I held her at arm's length, looking into her blue eyes with the now-red rims.

"Honey, this is something you're going to have to get from God for yourself. Directly. I'm sorry, but I can't help you."

It was hard to do, but I walked out of the room and left her alone.

Darlene did hear from God for herself. I came back later to find her beaming. "Loren, the Lord has spoken to me from the story of David and Abigail. Abigail said she would wash the feet of her husband's servants. That's my ministry. I'm to be a servant—a footwasher!"

It sounded like so little, especially from a strong woman like Dar, but she was happy and I couldn't help but be happy for her too. I held Dar close and thought of what this really meant. Darlene was the first of many who would be called full-time to YWAM but each individual would have to find his or her own niche. Ministry didn't have to fit some long-held stereotype: God had a unique work for each one. And each person had to hear it from God directly—not just accept my word for what He was saying.

Dar and I both knew that the basic thing was an attitude of heart. Dar had gotten that right. Really right.

After Singapore I watched her carrying out her ministry of "footwashing." When she saw a harassed missionary's wife, she'd jump in and do the dishes, insisting the lady spend some time with her children. Dar also shined at making whatever room we stayed in into our "home"—she'd pick some wildflowers and stick them in a jar, if nothing else. And I saw that her serving ministry went in another, very important direction. She sensed people's needs and answered their questions, spending time with them one-on-one, hearing them out, planting ideas, giving counsel. I was so glad that God had given me Darlene before this first big project of the Bahamas. The Summer of Service was going to be quite an undertaking. The first big wave of young people would soon be going out. An excitement began to churn in me. I could hardly wait to get to the Bahamas!

It was a dampish, chilly February evening in 1964, several months later, and Dad had a stack of logs crackling in their flagstone fireplace by the big windows overlooking the San Gabriel Valley. Except for Jannie, who was away at college in Springfield, Missouri, the whole family was there, including Phyllis and Len's two children, who were busy with blocks in the kitchen.

Dar and I were talking so excitedly even dear Mom didn't have a chance to get a word in edgewise.

"We'll have 30 islands as our target," I said, spreading a map of the Caribbean on the living room floor in front of the fireplace, pointing to a string of dots arcing from Florida toward the Dominican Republic. "We'll try to get to all the out islands with our English-speaking kids and to the Dominican Republic with Spanish-speaking kids. We'll be there two months." (I was glad we'd worked out our dates so that we'd be leaving before the heavy hurricane season.) We would fly from Miami to Nassau on the first of July, just five months from now. From there teams would take mail boats to the out islands. The Summer of Service would cost each participant $160 for two months, including airfare from Miami to Nassau and back.

"That's twenty dollars a week, son," Mother said. "Either this is of the Lord or you're crazy." She tapped her head.

We all laughed, but knowing Mom, she wasn't joking.

Dar and I kept the road hot recruiting. We went wherever we were invited. "The Summer of Service will be a rugged boot camp of faith," we told young people. "There will be health risks so you'll have to get approval from your parents and a doctor. You'll also need a recommendation from your pastor. But you'll have a chance to make a big difference in lives." We told them they would have to raise the $160 themselves, just as Dar and I were doing, and that it would be all work with no time off for sightseeing, no spending money that would make us "richer" than the islanders. "There won't even be dating while we are on the mission," I said.

The tougher we made the conditions, the more the kids volunteered.

As July 1 drew near, we prayed even harder to be led to the right people. Sometimes our prayers were answered in an unmistakable way. We were in Colorado and I was speaking to several hundred about our trip when I noticed one boy in particular. He was about eighteen. He had stick-straight, brown hair and was watching me intently.

I learned later that Dar, who was sitting in the crowd, heard God tell her to speak to a "boy in a green sweater" about coming on the Summer of Service. As soon as the meeting was over she made a beeline for the same boy—he was wearing a green sweater. She related to him what God had told her minutes before. The youth was dumbfounded. He kept hitting his chest with his open palm. "Uh, I . . . I just asked God to have one of you speak to me personally if He wanted me to go!" He fixed a straight gaze at Dar and then grinned. Dar grabbed his hand, pumping it up and down. "What's your name?" she asked the boy. "Don. Don Stephens."

I had to wonder what special role this Don Stephens might have with YWAM, given this most unusual way of being introduced to him.

On one of our recruiting trips Dar and I visited my sister Jannie at Evangel College. Jannie introduced her boyfriend, a slim, wavy-haired Oklahoman named Jimmy Rogers. We sat in our motel room near the college and told Jannie and Jimmy all about Summer of Service. Jannie's response was immediate. "This is just what I've always wanted—something *important* to do!" Jimmy wasn't as demonstrative but I could tell by his questions that he was on the hook too. Good! I liked the young man.

As we got closer to July 1, I suddenly realized Dar and I

didn't have the money for our own fees—$320 for the two of us. So I sold our VW bug. We were scrambling now to get everything done—like buying the three used school buses. We'd use them for the trek from California to Dallas, where we'd pick up more youths, going on to Florida to catch our flight on Mackey Airlines.

One week before our flight to Nassau, our three school buses, piled with suitcases and loaded with volunteers, began making their way to Florida. Dad called to tell me that at the last minute Phyllis and Len had decided to come along to help us with logistics. "And, son," Dad added, his encouragement and humor coming through the line, "your mother has a word for you again."

"What's that, Dad?"

"She says to remind you that either this is God's idea or you're crazy. And Loren. . . ."

"Yes, Dad?"

"I agree."

We both laughed. But in fact it was a serious observation. We could be out of our minds. On the other hand it was possible, just possible, that we were unleashing a power that we ourselves scarcely understood.

Chapter Eight

Blue Waters, Troubled Waters

Our buses picked up young people as we drove across the country until we had 146 volunteers for the summer—including 16 Spanish-speaking kids who were headed for the Dominican Republic. From Miami we flew to Nassau. I smiled, looking behind me at our convoy driving down Nassau's spacious boulevards: kids were crammed into cars and vans; more were sitting atop suitcases on a flatbed truck. They had responded from many different churches, all over North America. We were underway at last.

During the days of orientation at Evangelistic Temple I saw that two young men were making themselves especially useful. One was Jannie's nineteen-year-old friend Jimmy Rogers (who was already having his style crimped with the no-dating rule) and the other was eighteen-year-old Don Stephens—the green-sweatered kid from Colorado (whose style was crimped in the same way since his blond girlfriend, Deyon, was with us, too). I got to know Don right away and liked him a lot. His lithe build showed the toughening of outdoor life on the western slopes of Colorado. He found things that needed doing and simply did them. In Jimmy and Don both, were we looking at boys who would one day grow to be full-time YWAMers?

The orientation over, we prepared to move out for eight weeks of work. We divided into 25 all-boy and all-girl teams averaging six members each, and then shuttled our first group of four boys to dockside to catch the mail boat for one of the out islands. The sun beat down on us as we unloaded the van. Suitcases went aboard the little boat with the peeling paint as it bobbed up and down at its mooring. Then we stowed boxes of literature, a campstove and bedrolls.

Finally it was time for our YWAMers themselves to climb

aboard. One by one the four youths manfully shook my hand, then lumbered across the gangplank to perch atop large stalks of bananas.

"How long will it take for you to get to the Island?" I called to the captain.

He wiped his hands on his dirty uniform. "I don't know, *mon*, maybe 24 hours if the seas be kind!"

Then they were pulling away, the guys atop the bananas were laughing and waving. I waved back.

There were 24 more teams to get off—to Andros, where Don Stephens' team was headed; to Long Island where Jimmy Rogers would lead a group of seventeen; to Eleuthera where Jannie's team was assigned; to Grand Bahama where Don Stephens' blond girlfriend was leading a group. We would have six weeks to talk to every person on thirty out islands about Jesus Christ, followed by two weeks visiting homes in Nassau.

After we had shipped off the last team, Dar and I set out to visit as many as possible on the Bahamas and Dominican Republic. In one place, we arrived on our mail boat, clambered up onto the dock and were met by six exuberant girls. They helped us with our bags and bedrolls and brought us to their "home," an old, wooden schoolhouse with windows propped open by sticks. A dusty portrait of Queen Elizabeth gazed down on us primly from above the scratched blackboard.

"How are you gals doing?" Dar asked. Great, they replied. They had already gone to almost every home on the cay and were especially excited about the young people who were coming to their nightly open-air meetings in front of the store. "It's the only place with a generator, so we can have light."

On our next stop we got similar reports. The youths were in fact very good evangelists. As we went from island to island, Dar's and my euphoria grew like a bubble. I wanted to remember the details, especially when I told the leaders in Springfield about it.

-In one place a bartender made his decision to follow Christ and put his bar up for sale.

-An old man with a withered arm stretched his arm out, healed. The eighteen-year-old who prayed for him was so surprised she fainted.

-A woman who was almost totally blind began, for the first time in years, to read.

-A man with a painful, stiffened back was bending over and touching his toes, laughing.

-A boys' team hired a wizened fisherman to take them to an island in a small boat even though there was a squall. The boys prayed and the white-capped water smoothed in front of them. The amazed man ran ahead when they landed, calling people to come hear the young "men of God."

Dar and I went out to the Bahamian homes with the teams. I sat in one home on a rickety chair, watching as my partner, a teenage boy, prayed with a lady. The cracks in the wall of the shanty were so wide I could look outside to the dusty street. The woman accepted Jesus into her life, which was the purpose for our being there. But what excited me almost equally was the light of enthusiasm in the eyes of my teenaged partner as he handed the woman her very first Bible and promised he would pray for her and her family. When we left that shack with the wide cracks in the wall, I knew that neither the woman nor the boy would ever be the same again.

Six weeks flew by and the 130 young people boarded mail boats for their return to Nassau and our final two weeks in the capital city.

We were housed in an old Royal Air Force hangar on the outskirts of town. It leaned in disrepair beside the cracked cement of runways used during World War II. To the left of the cavernous entrance were rooms for the girls; the boys were on the right; Dar and I found a place for ourselves which doubled as a small storage room. We lined up the camp stoves and Jannie and Deyon were soon getting up at five o'clock each morning, organizing the cooking.

As we prepared for our last few days in Nassau we reviewed the records the kids had been keeping. Some 6,000 people had shown their interest in following Christ. Two churches were starting in the out islands as a result of the efforts of the young people. But the best results were not given in statistics, but experiences. Like the time when two YWAMers stopped a man who was headed into a bar with his hand in the pocket of his sportcoat. He stood and listened to them, then suddenly broke down and with tears in his eyes gave himself to Jesus. Then he showed the kids what was in his pocket—a gun. He had been headed into the bar to kill his wife. Instead, the YWAMers and the man went into that bar, found his wife and also brought her to faith in Christ. The man and his wife began coming to one of the local churches.

Our plan was to hold a city-wide rally in Nassau proper just before we flew out for the mainland. We started the meetings, continuing to visit the city's homes too, but with every passing day I wondered if we could finish the summer. I began to cast worried eyes on the horizon where ominous clouds were building. There were reports of tropical depressions that could bring severe weather. Then it began. Every night (always at the *end* of our rallies!) the skies opened and torrents were unleashed. The kids were ferried back to the hangar in an open truck; they were drenched but having a great time, singing loudly when they weren't sneezing. I was aware of potential danger even though the kids were blithely unaware. I looked around the ramshackle airplane hangar, now with water pouring through in several places.

What an introduction for young people to evangelism! It was a nightmare, and it was getting worse. On August 22, I heard that the first fully-formed hurricane of the season—Cleo—was boiling across the Atlantic. I rushed to the weather bureau and spoke to the man in charge. "Mister," he said, "if there was any way of getting my family out in time, I sure would do so." The storm had smashed through the French West Indies, then Haiti and the Dominican Republic where, (we held a praise session for the news) all sixteen of our Spanish-speaking YWAMers were safe. It was now in Cuba and it could be coming straight to Nassau!

I hurried back to evacuate the hangar—we took everyone to the solid, low-lying concrete Evangelistic Temple. The girls filled the basement rooms with air mattresses; the boys slept between the pews of the sanctuary upstairs. Dar and I took over the little office.

And we waited.

Outside, the winds were howling and water was pounding against the tightly shut louvered glass windows. We got together in the sanctuary and began to pray not so much for ourselves, because we felt safe, but for the people we'd met in squatters' shacks in the slums of Nassau, and in the derelict houses teetering in village after village on the out islands. I especially remembered the home where I could look at the street through cracks in the wall.

That night, there in the church with the storm battering the island, I realized that many of us were in danger of not stressing properly one major part of the Gospel message. Jesus told us there were two important things to do. One was to love God with all our hearts, souls, minds and strength—teaching people to do that *is* evangelism. The other command was to love our neighbors as ourselves—to take care of people, as much as is in our power to do. These were two sides of the same Gospel: loving God and loving neighbor. The two should be almost indistinguishable—so linked that it would be hard to tell them apart.

My heart kept pace with the pounding wind and rain. I was sensing a whole new concept in missions taking shape—combining evangelism with acts of mercy.

The next day, two feet of water ran down Bay Street, Nassau's main thoroughfare, but the strength of the storm had missed us. Darlene and I were in our little office-bedroom when a stocky young volunteer came in with a report.

"I just heard on my radio, Loren, that Hurricane Cleo has killed at least 138 people. It has injured hundreds more and left thousands without homes!"

I looked at Dar and knew that she too was thinking of the shantytowns and the people we had met on the primitive out islands. "Let's pray," I suggested. Darlene and I and the young YWAMer bowed our heads and prayed for people who had lost what little they had, those who were without homes, those who had lost family.

"I just wish there were something we could *do*," I said. "If we could go in with food, clothing, building supplies—we could even have our fellows help rebuild homes. But to handle so many people, so many tons of supplies, we'd need a ship."

Even as I spoke an idea began to take shape in my mind.

It would be a great thing, wouldn't it! A ship for going to places of real need. A ship filled with kids who could help people in practical ways *and* tell them about Jesus as the ultimate answer to their problems.

But it was a pipe dream, wasn't it? Certainly, for now, there was nothing much we could do since we were leaving. It was a frustration. We helped clean up the church then packed our bags to return home. But as we did so I knew something had been planted in my spirit. We Christians needed to reach out, as Jesus did, into areas of people's lives where they *felt* they were hurting. All too often we just let slide this expression of God's caring.

Yes, something had been sown in my spirit by Hurricane Cleo. I wondered how long it would be before the seed began to germinate.

The eight weeks of Summer of Service were over. We put the kids on the plane for Miami. They had done a great job. There had been close calls but everyone was doing well. Finally it was time for us, too, to go home. We were bone weary as we drove to the airport, but we knew, really knew, that this had been God's idea.

Waves of young people were going out. We had come very close to our goal of seeing every person reached on thirty out islands and many hundreds more contacted in Nassau. I couldn't wait to report to the leaders in Springfield.

Dar and I breezed back home totally unprepared for the cold reception that hit us there.

Chapter Nine

The Key to "Releases"

Darlene and I pulled our VW van away from my folks' house where we had been living and headed east toward Springfield. The late November weather was not likely to be good as we drove toward Missouri, but it couldn't be worse than we'd known in Hurricane Cleo. Dar and I had a lot of mixed emotions as we left the folks' house that morning. We were sad because of news from Aunt Sandra: just a few days ago we learned that she had cancer. We all called back immediately to assure her that we were praying. How glad I was that eight years ago I had decided to try getting back in touch with family while on that singing tour in Miami!

On a happier note was the upcoming visit with the General Superintendent of the Assemblies of God, Thomas Zimmerman. I could just imagine his excitement when we outlined to him what we'd been discovering, that the church could in fact guide young people into effective evangelistic work. Our dream was actually working! We had opened YWAM to all denominations but we still wanted to stay within the framework of the Assemblies.

We'd driven straight through. Darlene was very tired and stayed in the motel room which we'd rented near Jannie's college so that we could visit with her and Jimmy later. "There'll be plenty of time for getting together with the people at headquarters, honey," Dar said.

So I was alone as I bounded across the marble lobby and pushed the button for the third floor. I stepped out into the hushed, carpeted executives' domain. These men had all sacrificed in their youth, pastoring congregations like the one that met in a blacksmith shop during my folks' early years. So they'd be open to pioneering. Reports from the Bahamas would have reached them by now. They'd know what a great job the kids had done.

The secretary ushered me into the superintendent's office. "Hello, Brother Zimmerman. . . ." *Brother* was a special term of respect in our denomination meant to underline the fact that we were brothers and sisters in God's family. Brother Zimmerman shook my hand cordially then sat down and looked at me across his desk. Indeed he had heard about the Bahamian experiment. But if I were expecting a quick endorsement and a blank check to work interdenominationally and still maintain my standing as a minister with my church, I was mistaken. The problem, I gathered as we sat talking quietly, was that new works like ours needed to be brought under the organizational umbrella—not outside and autonomous. There was a place for me in the Assemblies, but of course I would have to be a full team player. In the end I was offered a job. A good one, too, there at headquarters, complete with a fine salary, a staff, a budget. "You can continue with your vision, Loren, but you'd be taking out a more manageable number—say ten or twenty young people a year."

My heart dropped to my knees as the very gracious offer came out—it sounded so reasonable, so secure. Only it was far from what I believed God had told me to do: send out waves of young people from all denominations into evangelism. I tried to explain what I had felt God was saying to me about what was about to happen. It was much, much bigger than twenty a year, and larger than any one denomination. "Sir," I said, "there's another generation coming. It's different from anything we've ever seen—"

I floundered, for I could hear how foolish it sounded. Brother Zimmerman assured me he had worked with young people for decades and knew them well. As he tried to explain his reservations about my plans, I could truly see his dilemma. If I had his responsibility of leading a large movement, I would need submitted people—ready to play by the rules for the good of the whole. But here I was, hearing a different drummer, out of step. That's more or less what Brother Zimmerman said, too. He was sorry but I'd have to leave the team—resign—if I couldn't play by the rules.

"God, is this really You?" I said quickly to myself. And I

thought I heard the answer that it was indeed His leading. I knew what I had to do. If I was really *sure* what God was telling me, then I had to obey and accept the consequences. Brother Zimmerman agreed, but he had no choice either.

I shook hands with Brother Zimmerman, thanked him and walked slowly, heavily back to the elevator, back across the marble floor, back out the door aware even as I walked that this would be forever. I was churning inside, confused about what had happened.

It was a sober time back in the motel room. Jimmy and Jannie had come over. As we discussed what had happened the enormity of my decision settled over us.

"People will think I was kicked out," I said.

"And preachers don't usually lose their credentials except for fooling around with women, or getting caught with their hands in the till or having screwy doctrine!" Jannie pointed out.

"What I dread is telling my folks," Dar said. My heart dropped a little lower. I looked at Jimmy, leaning forward in his chair, cradling his chin in a hand propped on one knee. I knew he was thinking about his own parents, too.

For a long quiet moment we just sat there. I was going over again and again what had happened. I clamped my jaw tightly. I was committed not to rebel but a germ of resentment was settling in.

Back in California, the word was out. I was no longer a minister with the Assemblies of God. It was difficult for Darlene and me; it was difficult for our families. But I knew that I had done the right thing. Ever since I had preached my first sermon as a thirteen-year-old on testing, I had gone through these challenges. I had turned down the offer of potential wealth from Aunt Sandra, given up my reputation in my denomination and settled for a risky and presumptuous-sounding call to send out waves of young missionaries.

After Jesus was tested in the wilderness, His ministry was released. Now I looked forward to the future. It seemed like we were poised on the launchpad, waiting for the lift-off.

One event took place about eight months after our Bahamian experience which had a strange, bittersweet quality about it: Aunt Sandra was dying.

I made a special trip back east just to see her after her surgery. When she met me at the Providence airport, it didn't seem possible that she had a vicious breast cancer. Her face was still beautiful, though paler and thinner, her hair was carefully done, her fingers faultlessly manicured. She wore a yellow suit, and you couldn't detect the disfigurement of her surgery.

"Loren, darling!" She kissed me on the cheek, took my arm and showed me to her limousine outside. As we drove along the streets of Providence with the trees bursting with spring green, I brought her up to date, filling her in on our future hopes.

"And how are you, Aunt Sandra?"

Aunt Sandra leaned back. "I've started going to this church, Loren. I'd like you to see it tomorrow, if we have time."

I certainly did. The next day Aunt Sandra and I drove up to a colonial brick Baptist church with columns on the front. We found the big double doors unlocked and went inside to the hushed coolness. A glow from the tall windows bathed the empty pews. Aunt Sandra pointed to the choir loft. "I sing in the choir now, Loren. It helps when I feel I'm doing something for the church."

She had not, I noticed, said she was singing for the Lord. I knew the time had come to do something very important. My aunt was dying and she was trying to do what was right. I had to tell her how to receive forgiveness for her sins—how to come to Jesus Christ.

We slipped into one of the back pews and I just plunged ahead. "Aunt Sandra, wouldn't you like to make a commitment of your life to Jesus Christ?"

"Oh, yes, Loren!" she said, her eyes brimming.

I spoke the phrases of a simple prayer. Aunt Sandra repeated the words after me, giving herself to God and to His care.

"Dear Jesus, I do accept you as my Lord and Savior. Come into my life now and forgive me for my sins."

I left her and I knew somehow it would be the last time I saw her in this world.

It was not easy getting back in the swing of our work at YWAM partly because I found myself thinking often of my aunt, but partly too, I had to confess, because I was still feeling off balance after my visit to Springfield. We were totally on our own now, without the sponsorship of a large denomination. As I looked into the future I had no way at all of guessing that the launchpad we'd been looking for would turn out to be located in a tiny country halfway around the earth called New Zealand.

It was January, but this was summertime in the Southern Hemisphere and the sun beat down as the small seaplane flew toward my destination, a rugged campsite on an island off the coast of New Zealand. I thought back over the past six years since YWAM had started. Twenty-two vocational volunteers had gone out during our first experimental years, then a tangible glimpse of my larger dream was realized when 146 went out to the Bahamas and the Dominican Republic. Each year after that additional volunteers went out during school vacations. The waves were rising very gradually as we sent kids into the West Indies, Samoa and Hawaii, Mexico and Central America. Yet it still seemed we were missing something. "Why do we have so few workers?" I asked Darlene before leaving her to come on this trip. Four and a half years after our marriage, we had hundreds of short-term volunteers each summer but there were only eight full-time workers besides Dar and me. I yearned to see something I could only call a *releasing*—some tangible evidence that God was really in this dream. Maybe New Zealand would hold the answers.

Now our seaplane circled the sparkling sea, dipping to a rocky inlet on the island off New Zealand, Great Barrier. The remote campsite, curling around the water's edge at the foot of steep, pine-scattered hills, consisted of a few old buildings, a large patched meeting tent and some smaller sleeping tents. In this camp of Christians we intended to recruit for a YWAM outreach in the South Pacific.

Our plane skimmed the water creating a spectacular spray that obscured my vision. Jannie and Jimmy, her husband of five months, had come out ahead of me and were waiting for me now. They met me at the rocky beach. With them was a couple in their early forties with whom I felt immediately at home. Jim Dawson was an urbane businessman, clad in the camp attire of shorts and sandals. His wife Joy's warm and bubbly patter spilled over as they led me to my accommodations. For my two-week stay I was given one of the "luxury rooms" in a line of whaler's shacks.

There were about 150 at the campsite and we were telling them about our new idea of taking young people out in missions. After two weeks here on Great Barrier we would have a week of visiting homes in a section of the New Zealand city, Auckland. Then we hoped some would join us in the South Pacific Region.

I had come as a speaker but it turned out that I was the one who was learning new ideas on this isolated island. The first came from the New Zealand kids themselves. They had a guidance practice which intrigued me. In their minds they would be "given" a chapter and verse from the Bible without knowing what the reference said; then they would consider whether or not that reading was a special guidance. "You'd be surprised how often God uses that as a way to speak," they insisted. The key, they said, was being totally submitted to the Spirit of Jesus; if He wanted to speak He could use any tool He chose, including this quite mysterious one.

There were other surprises when I was invited to pray with the camp leaders. There were five of us, including the camp director and Jim and Joy Dawson. Four of us were to be speakers, including Joy, but today we were going to pray over the *order* of the speakers. What I expected was a time of general prayer then a discussion. Instead, one of the people explained to me as a first-timer that in this kind of practical guidance-prayer they would ask God to tell each person individually exactly the same thing. I tried to hid my astonishment.

Okay, I thought bemusedly, *let's see what happens. Who should be the speaker today, Lord?*

I bowed my head along with the others and asked God. I confess that some not-so-spiritual thoughts flitted through my mind. *What if I'm the only one who doesn't hear a thing? Or what if I get some idea that's off the wall?* But the people around me were experienced Christians and they were all fully expecting God to speak separately, giving each the same answer. So I decided I'd trust God, too. I leaned back in my folding chair but inside I was on the edge of my seat, waiting to see what would happen.

Then that familiar voice inside my mind said a name—one of the four around me.

"Well," said the camp director, "is everybody ready?"

One by one each of us spoke out the name that had come into his mind. Each of us had heard the same thing! Five different people, yet each had the same answer. A breeze fluttered through an open window, heightening the shiver of excitement I felt inside.

Day after day we found specific guidance in this same way. I was fascinated. The other four leaders had been praying together like this for years. Yet I felt we were on the same team. I really belonged.

Then one day our prayer-plan didn't seem to work. We were meeting outside, so we could soak up the sun while taking care of business. But this time, when we prayed some felt I was to be the speaker, some believed it was to be Joy Dawson.

I was curious to see what had gone wrong. Obviously someone hadn't heard correctly, I thought.

"Looks like we need to go back to the Lord," Joy stated matter-of-factly. She told us that she and Jim had learned that sometimes this happens and you need to ask God if there's another factor you don't understand. So we bowed our heads for "Round Two" and asked God for clarification. Then the understanding came to each of us—it was not Loren *or* Joy, but *both*. First Joy, then me. This really was amazing, I thought to myself. It was like the Three Wise Men. They each followed the star—their individual perception of God's direction—and doing so, came together to be led to Jesus.

It was time to leave for the house-to-house work in Auckland. We had a lot to do to get ready for the special week ahead. I felt myself getting revved up, the way I used to feel at exam times at graduate school in USC. And I knew how little time I had for the work I had to do.

I was also still looking for the *releases* we had been waiting for.

Perhaps there would be something I would learn in Auckland—some secrets of guidance I did not yet grasp—to bring those releases, to unleash the waves.

"Father," I prayed, as our little passenger ferry was leaving Great Barrier Island for the long trip to Auckland, "I'm trying to learn to listen. Please help me to see the next step You have in mind."

An hour later, standing at the rail with the cold spray misting my face, I found myself thinking again of the story I had used for my first sermon. Jesus had been in the wilderness, fasting and praying just before the beginning—the releasing—of His work on earth. I saw a pattern in this story from Jesus' life, but I tried to shrug it off. Could it be that God wanted me to give up food for a while and pray? I opened a door to the idea. "God, do You want me to go on a fast?"

Immediately the answer rushed into my brain. "Yes, and I want you to withdraw from people for seven days. Starting when you arrive."

I was dumbfounded. There was so much to *do!* "Am I hearing you right, God?" I asked again. Withdrawing from people meant I'd shirk my duties, let Jim and Jannie do the work of preparing for our outreach, the very thing we'd come thousands of miles to do. "Is that really You?" The only answer I got was another quiet voice saying, "The Dawsons are going to ask you to stay with them. Say yes."

Well, that invitation was unlikely to come because the Dawsons knew I planned to stay elsewhere. If it *did* come, I could see God's hand more clearly. I'd know He wanted me to fast and pray. Even if it meant leaving an "unfair" amount of work on Jim and Jannie.

I said nothing about all of this to anyone, just waited to see what would happen. The sea and the sky darkened to evening.

Then, just as the lights of Auckland began to glimmer on the horizon, Jim Dawson joined me at the rail. I held my breath as Jim began to speak. He seemed hesitant. "Uh, Loren, uh, I know you're planning to stay with other friends but Joy and I, well, we believe we've heard something from the Lord. Would you stay with us?"

Chapter Ten

Coming to God with a Clean Heart

I glanced around the Dawsons' two-story Scandinavian style home with its breathtaking panorama of the harbor.

Jim ushered me downstairs to their guestroom. It was simply furnished, comfortable and secluded, with its own outside entrance. I remembered God's words that I was to "withdraw from people." I called Jimmy and Jannie to give them the bad news that I couldn't help them for a week.

"Well, you have to do what you feel is right, Loren," Jimmy said in his slow Oklahoma drawl. I could imagine his thoughts. *What do you mean we won't see you for seven days? You're going to fast while we do all the work?* But Jimmy said nothing like this. He was too loyal. That made it all the worse.

After I hung up the phone I knelt on the green carpet beside my bed. Yes, this was exactly what I should be doing. Praying. In some as-yet-unseen way this time apart was important to work itself. All my life I'd heard about holiness. Well, holiness was probably another way of saying have the right priorities in your life. And for me, this week, getting alone with God, was *the* priority. I couldn't help but wonder, too, if this week weren't directly involved with guidance.

The first two days were uneventful. I would get down on my knees and pray, walk around the room and pray, sit down and pray, stretch full-length on the floor and pray. There was also lots of leisure for reading my Bible. But most of the time I just waited. Sometimes God would speak a word or two; at other times, we enjoyed a companionable silence.

It was the third day of the fast before the breakthrough came. The only word I can use to describe what happened to me is *surgery*. It was like soul surgery.

I was lying face down on the carpet, waiting on God. Suddenly a sharp scalpel of conscience probed.

"Remember Springfield?"

Faster than I could imagine, attitudes began to surface. Critical feelings and resentment towards my denominational leaders who hadn't seen the vision of YWAM the way that I did—especially my brother, Thomas Zimmerman. For two years now, since I reported to Springfield after the Bahamas, I'd been smarting under the rejection, and in my heart I'd begun to deny my own roots.

I suddenly saw all the time I had wasted, trying to defend myself and my ideas. That time was robbed from the real work that needed to be done, talking to people about Jesus.

Crying, I asked for mercy. From now on I'd speak out in real praise for my former leaders, grateful again for them and for my heritage. I'd let God defend the vision, it if was from Him. Lying there on the green carpet, I knew that God had heard me and forgiven me.

The scalpel probed again. And again. Throughout the day, hour after hour. My pride suddenly loomed before me—I saw the times I had acted for the recognition of men rather than God. Mom's words in my bedroom-turned-office dropped into my mind: "Son, if you get proud, God can't use you." Then God put His finger on sins of the mind, sexual fantasies. As each sin—of thought, or attitude, or action—came to my mind, I confessed it, asking God to forgive me and help me to turn away from it.

When I knew the soul surgery was over, there was one more thing to be done. I found stationery and a pen and began the first of several letters I knew I had to write, making things right with people. "Dear Brother Zimmerman, . . . " It was excruciating, but that night I settled back into bed with a brand new feeling of cleanness. On my desk in the little room was a tidy pile of letters. The one on top was addressed to Springfield, Missouri.

By the end of the week as I began to come slowly off my fast, I realized that I—and perhaps YWAM—had just passed a turning point common to all who seek to hear the voice of God. We can hear the Lord more clearly if we come to Him with a clean heart. The process of confession was an ongoing one, to be sure. But I'd made a good start.

I wondered what would come of it!

The very first event to follow was certainly not good. Jim Rogers had protected me during my week of prayer but promptly on the seventh day he called with the news. We had shipped 100,000 booklets to New Zealand to give out in the homes and on the streets. They had arrived during my fast and had been stored in a factory basement. A rainstorm had flooded that basement, and all of our booklets were soaked.

"Could you come right over, Loren?" Jim gave the address.

Half an hour later I made my way down the factory stairs to the damp basement. Jimmy met me and just swept his arms out. Jannie and three other volunteers were pulling thousands of waterlogged booklets out of soggy boxes and stacking them in piles on a huge table.

"I think we can salvage them, Loren," said Jannie. She took me to see a huge industrial press. The booklets were placed in the press and much of the water squeezed out. Then one by one the booklets were strung on clotheslines to dry. What a beginning to our famous Auckland effort.

Surprisingly, though, all of our spirits were high. We spent the week drying books on clotheslines, then on Saturday morning we drove to a sleazy downtown address. "Don't you wish Mom could see us now, sis?" I asked Jannie, laughing, as we parked in front of the Pink Pussycat Club. The Christian coffeehouse which we were using as a headquarters was in a basement next door to the Pink Pussycat. We unloaded boxes of almost-dry booklets and took them downstairs to the black-and-red hall where free coffee and inexpensive sandwiches were served to street people from the neighborhood.

In groups of four and five, volunteers drifted in until there were thirty people downstairs in the black-and-red room. I looked at the guys, still in their teens, dressed in popular narrow Continental trousers, and at the girls with their miniskirts and square-toed shoes. My eyes were especially drawn to one teenage guy with a broad Polynesian face and a carefree grin. (Why did he seem to stand out in this group?) Among these thirty young people, could I be looking at future missionaries? Would these same kids some day find themselves in the Philippines or West Africa, or even in countries behind the Iron Curtain?

I took a deep breath and started in, speaking of our reason for coming to Auckland, giving the plan of action. We were going into Ponsonby, a Polynesian ghetto where thousands of Maoris, Samoans, Tongans and Cook Islanders lived. Over a map we blocked out a large area enclosing hundreds of homes. Again, the youth with the broad Polynesian face seemed to separate himself from the crowd. He asked bright, pointed questions. "You couldn't have picked a harder neighborhood," he said.

"I expect you're right. What's your name?"

"Kalafi Moala."

I found I was making note of the name.

Kalafi Moala was right about Ponsonby. It was a tough area. After a cheerless day of almost constant rebuffs, we gathered back at the basement coffeehouse for a debriefing. "I almost caught pneumonia from the draft of doors slamming in my face!" Jannie said.

The next day, Kalafi was my partner. As we walked between rows of once-grand Victorian homes, whose gardens were now weed-filled and littered with beer cans, I picked up pieces of information about this young man. Kalafi was eighteen, the eldest son of nine children. Tonga, his home, was a Polynesian monarchy—tiny archipelago two thousand miles to the east between Fiji and Samoa.

Like most Tongans, Kalafi had been raised to go to church but there was no living relationship between him and God. Apparently he was a natural leader in Tonga's most prestigious school, but also a drinking, carousing troublemaker. -

Kalafi went on to say that in the wee hours one morning when he had come home drunk, he suddenly saw the wasteland his life was becoming. He knelt beside his bed and began to cry.

74

He wept for three hours, asking God to come into his life and change him. He got off his knees at eight o'clock, a new young man. Kalafi told me how, before he graduated, he and his friends were meeting regularly to pray and read the Bible. Many of the students at his school became Christians.

The first day we had gone into Ponsonby had been almost fruitless. Today was different. When Kalafi, as a Polynesian, spoke to others from the islands, he got through. People listened, especially when he didn't "preach" but just told his own story of God's power to change. As the day wore on I began to hope, secretly, that young Kalafi would be part of the release I was praying for.

I didn't have to wait long. One night in the coffeehouse toward the end of our week, Kalafi said he wanted to talk to me. We found a corner. Above the blare of music Kalafi came straight to the point.

"Loren, I think we need a YWAM team to come to Tonga." Kalafi told me that next July, five months away, would be the coronation of Tonga's new king, Taufa'ahau Tupou IV. Thousands of Tongans would be pouring into the capital city of Nuku'alofa. "I think it would be an ideal time for you people to be there," Kalafi said.

Then he added, "And I'll work with you—full-time. I've decided to give up my plans—and they were pretty good ones, Loren. I'll go back to Tonga instead and make arrangements for the teams."

I looked at Kalafi, suddenly excited. I knew about his excellent career potential and was more than a little awed at what he was sacrificing. This was what we needed if ever we were to grow: young men and women who would hear and obey God's voice for themselves and move out.

"Yes, let's do it!" I said. It was right. That same night, with the walls vibrating from the loud music, we prayed for Tonga.

When I went home to the Dawsons' late that night, I thought that possibly Kalafi was our first new leader from the non-Western world. It didn't escape me either that he had been released after my days of cleansing and fasting and praying.

My six weeks in New Zealand were over. As I mounted the steps to the plane that would take me to Darlene—we had planned to meet in Hawaii for a second honeymoon—I reflected on how much had happened in this short time. We'd had a successful outreach into a ghetto. And the releasing had begun. Besides Kalafi, there were at least seven others whom I saw as probable future leaders for us. It hit me: eight people! In six weeks' time the number of full-timers in YWAM had possibly doubled.

But, even so, we were still adding to our numbers one by one. Someday I envisioned being able to grow not by *addition* but by multiplication. Multiplication produced growth so much faster than addition. I thought again of Kalafi. If he were only trained properly he'd be able to train and send out other young people— especially people from the Third World.

The plane climbed above the clouds and settled in at 30,000 feet. I reflected that these past few weeks had been like a school. I'd been taught guidance principles by people who knew new ways of hearing God. Then I'd put these principles to work. Really, it wasn't much different from growing up in our family. Darlene and I both had had such incredibly rich childhoods of teaching and example from our parents and grandparents that in a way, we had an unfair advantage. Wouldn't it be great to have a school, deliberately designed to be in a family setting, where people could be introduced to these things and allowed the chance to try them out for themselves?

What a great idea! Maybe in fact it was God's idea! If so, perhaps I could see the Wise Men Principle at work which I'd just learned, where two or more people see the same guiding star at the same time. If this idea of a school for teaching the *ways* of the Lord really came from God, then it was reasonable to expect that He'd give it to more than one person. I would want to tell Darlene about it of course, but otherwise it would be wise to keep my next goal for YWAM a secret.

My plane arrived before Darlene's. As I stepped out of the air-conditioning of the cabin, there was that familiar caress of soft, warm air and the smell of the plumeria trees. I was so glad that we had decided to have this time alone in Hawaii before plunging back into work on the mainland. What was it about Hawaii that felt so right to me? I looked around at the mix of Oriental, Polynesian and Western faces. Hawaii really was a linkage point between East and West.

I had just enough time before Dar's arrival to rent a pink and white striped jeep. If we were going to have a second honeymoon, why not do it right?

Darlene came down the plane steps looking lovely in a blue dress with her blond hair carefully in place. I swept her into my arms in a crushing hug! We threw our suitcases into the pink jeep, and sped away to a small apartment, with the wind making a quick job of undoing Dar's careful coiffure.

I quickly brought her up to date on all that had happened in New Zealand: meeting the Dawsons and Kalafi, all about the terrible but wonderful spiritual surgery in the Dawsons' home and especially all the things I had been learning about guidance. Incredibly, Dar told me that she had been fasting and praying on the same exact days as I, and that she, too, had gone through soul surgery. It was amazing to see how God had been leading us together, though thousands of miles apart.

We were circling the island one lazy day and had stopped at the Blowhole, past Diamond Head. We parked the jeep and clambered down the black lava rocks. Below us, mammoth waves pounded into the ponderous boulders, crashing in and receding. Often a titan would roll in, rushing under some of these boulders, causing a sudden fountain to spurt through a hole in the rocks in a spectacular spray. We sat down on a cliff and watched. The enormous power of the water awed me. Again I pictured the waves of young people, and thought how they would need to know how to channel God's power.

There was one more, special thing I wanted to talk to Dar about, and this seemed the perfect place for it, with the surging waves concentrating beneath our feet.

"You know, Dar," I began, "there's something big on my mind. . . ." And I told her about the school.

"That's a great idea!" she said. "So many special people have been giving us the input we've needed lately. I'd love to see kids have the same opportunity!"

A mantle of tropical clouds gathered around the shoulders of the green mountains behind us as we excitedly began telling each other all our ideas for such a school: The kids would learn how to truly love God with all their hearts, souls, minds and bodies. They could have the chance to learn from special men and women who had been practicing what they were teaching. This floating faculty would come, one at a time, right from the center of action.

"And it could be in a family-type setting with all of us learning together—students and teachers." Dar suggested, reminding me how we had gotten so close with the young people living in the hangar in Nassau.

The kids would not only learn in the classroom, but through experience. They would be learning by doing—going to foreign countries, meeting people, seeing the conditions, helping.

Ideas began to fall over one another. We hammered out details for the school until I noticed the sun was an orange ball, dipping low over the horizon.

Before we left our spot on the cliff, I told Dar about the principle of keeping guidance a secret until God gives permission to share it. Perhaps this would be one of those times when He would show us through someone else that He was in this idea of a school.

We looked forward to a Christmas with the whole family at Mom and Dad's new apartment in Alhambra, California. Jim and Jannie were flying in from the South Pacific where I had left them ten months earlier. Dad would be as busy as usual overseeing churches and missionaries. Phyllis and her husband, Len, with their two children lived a few blocks away and it would be great seeing them. And of course, Mom would be there to spark the conversation with plenty of spice.

We walked in the front door of the apartment to the delicious smell of roasting turkey. Mom, flushed from her labors in the kitchen, gave us both a hug, then Dad enveloped us in his big arms, followed in a line by all the others.

I began to pump Jim and Jannie for details about the last ten months "down under." I was especially anxious to hear about Kalafi and Tonga. There was so much to say, Jim and Jannie were soon vying for a chance to speak. By the time they arrived with their 35 foreigners, Kalafi had recruited twenty Tongans to work with them.

People from all the islands had poured into the capital city for the coronation. The YWAMers had given out thousands of tracts. Everyone seemed to want one; nobody threw the tracts away. (I remembered all the refusals in Ponsonby.) Hundreds came to know Jesus.

"And Kalafi?" I asked.

"He did a great job," Jimmy said.

I thought to myself, *It really worked—it's multiplying now, without my even being there!* Now if Kalafi could only come to our school!

It was nearly time for our Christmas dinner and Mom was already clanging pots in the kitchen. Dar passed by me and gave me a meaningful look, and I knew she was thinking about the very special package she had slipped under the tree.

After dinner, we gathered in the living room to open our presents. Soon the floor was filled with crumpled paper and ribbon.

There remained only one large package with a tag reading, "To Mom from Loren and Darlene. HOLD UNTIL LAST." As it was placed on Mom's lap, I looked over at Dar—her eyes glittered.

Mom ripped open the box and with a puzzled look on her face pulled out a tiny Christmas stocking and a note which she read silently. Her jaw dropped, her eyes widened and she looked over at us. "Wow! You don't mean it?" gasped Mom, looking over at us with a sly grin.

"What is it, what does it say!" cried the others, almost in unison.

Finally, above the ruckus, Mom read aloud, "This little stocking is for you to fill next year. In July you will be having a third grandchild."

After five years of marriage, Dar and I felt it was the right time to start our family. Everyone started laughing, patting me on the back and shouting congratulations. Dad sat back in his recliner grinning.

"I'm glad you two finally stayed out of an airplane long enough to get one!"

The fall of 1967, several months after my return from New Zealand, I got the flu. Not very unusual, but what happened next was! While I was in bed in California, nursing my aches and fever, a thought came into my mind: "You *are* to have a school. It is to be called a School of Evangelism." I wondered if this were from God. The idea grew and I remembered the things Dar and I had talked about in Hawaii. Then another thought suddenly cut through, "Your school is to be in *Switzerland*."

Switzerland! "Is this you, God?" I asked in my mind. Sure, I remembered my visit to that lovely, alpine country. I had found it entrancing. But why there? We had done nothing in Europe—YWAMers had gone to Africa, the Caribbean, South Pacific, Latin America and Asia. But Europe?

I told Darlene about it and we made our plans to scout things out in Switzerland the following spring, using our "nest egg" house in La Puente as collateral for a loan to get the tickets. I still wondered, though, if this Switzerland idea were really from God. I wanted Him to reassure me that I had, in fact, been hearing from Him.

He did—in a striking way.

Two days before we were to leave, I got an unexpected invitation to breakfast. Dad and his friend, a Bible teacher named Willard Cantelon, had made a breakfast appointment. Willard called and insisted that Dad bring me along. "It's important," he said.

So Dad and I arrived at Foxey's Restaurant in Glendale to find Willard waiting for us in a horseshoe booth, dressed nattily in a tweed sportcoat, his homburg hat carefully placed aside. I shook his hand, curious to hear why he wanted me here.

Even afterwards as I reviewed what he said, I could not believe it.

"Loren, I have a message for you," Willard said. "The Lord has been planting the idea in my mind that someone should start a school in Switzerland. Last night He told me *you* are to be the one." I found my tongue and mumbled something. Willard went on to say that the school was to have an international student body and visiting teachers. "I'm not to be one of the teachers, Loren, I'm just a channel to pass this message on to you."

As Willard spoke, I, of course, found myself getting more and more excited. With this astonishing example of the Wise Men Principle at work, I now knew we were absolutely right in going to Switzerland.

We landed in Geneva in April. We drank in the sights of the green valleys surrounding Lake Geneva and boarded a crack train for Lausanne. What a sense of anticipation we felt as we zoomed past tranquil fields and storybook chalets and immaculate barns!

"Do you think this could ever feel like home?" I asked Dar.

"I love it!" she said. "I could stay here the rest of my life!"

We walked around Lausanne slowly, for Dar's sake, enjoying the flowers, the glitter of Lake Geneva, the twin steeples of the cathedral, the distant blue outline of the Alps. And all the while we marveled that God had told us to come here to start our school. We made arrangements for a facility in a town outside Lausanne and returned to the States to have our baby.

Dar's time for delivery was close, and I admit that Switzerland was not very much on my mind.

It was July 3, 1968. I was in Philadelphia and Darlene was in Redwood City, California, with her parents, waiting. The baby wasn't due for three weeks, but when I woke up that July morning I had a feeling I should call Dar. Her voice was excited.

"How would you like to be a daddy today?"

"Today!" All other business was immediately forgotten. "Are you sure?"

"Yes, I've already gone into labor," Dar said. "My guess is our baby will be born about eight or nine o'clock tonight."

"I'll be right there!" I half-shouted and hung up the phone.

But it was easier said than done. I finally got a seat booked on the busy eve of the Fourth of July holiday, only to sit for three hours on the runway of the Philadelphia airport before our plane was allowed to take off. I arrived at the hospital in Redwood City at eleven that night, frustrated and guilty that I hadn't been able to get there sooner.

I spotted Darlene's folks in the waiting room. "Am I too late?"

No, they assured me, but Darlene had been having a hard time. The doctor said the baby was coming breech—bottom first.

I rushed into the labor room. Darlene was lying limply on the pillow, alternately bearing down with all her body, then sinking again onto the sweat-dampened sheets.

"I had to wait for you," she gasped, smiling weakly between the sudden grimaces of contractions. I grasped her hand and sat beside her to wait and to pray.

The time came for them to wheel her into the delivery room. Finally, at three o'clock on the morning of the Fourth of July, the doctor breezed in, removing his mask and gloves to shake my hand.

"Congratulations! You have a beautiful baby girl! It was a difficult birth, but your wife was a real trouper!"

We named her Karen Joy. Now we were a real family. And we were looking forward to another birth: the school that seemed to hold so much promise for all the releases for which we had been longing.

Chapter Eleven

Multiplication of Guidance

Two years had passed since I first glimpsed God's strategy for a short-term school as part of His plan for sending young people out as missionaries. Not many of the kids we met had Dar's and my advantage of growing up in families which were really miniature schools. In our homes we'd learned the *ways* of God, how He purifies, how He provides, how He guides. God, I now felt, wanted that same experience for all YWAMers, especially those who were to be full-timers; and He showed us this by giving a special leading of the Wise Men Principle. He wanted a family-like school and it was to be in Switzerland.

It was hard to believe that it had been more than a year since we first came to Switzerland, looking for a place to have a school. The past year had been full of experimentation and false starts. The facility which we found for our school when we first came proved unsuitable. But just last week a friend spotted an old hotel, all boarded up. He thought it might be perfect for us so Dar and I walked over to investigate, pushing fourteen-month-old Karen in her stroller.

And there it was—a big old hotel—five stories tall, made of grayish stucco with old green shutters. It sat on a hill beside a dense evergreen forest. We walked all around it, onto the large lawn in front with an arbor of sycamore trees sheltering what once must have been an outdoor cafe. Across the roof was a weathered, painted sign, "Hotel Golf." ("There must be a golf course nearby," I commented.) We spent some time on the front lawn, enjoying the view of nearby pastures and cows with large bells ("Listen, Loren, you can hear the cowbells!") and of course, the majestic Alps looming on the horizon.

We found the owner in a two-story annex next to the main building. To our relief she spoke English. Yes, she would be interested in renting the hotel and yes, we could see it now. She produced some keys. "If you need anything, monsieur, please ask. The hotel, he has been boarded up for years, but everything is there."

Strangely aware that we might often be walking up those same front steps, I turned the key, pushed the stubborn door and we went in. A musty, dank smell met us. Fine cobwebs hung in the corners of the entryway. The lobby was furnished with shabby, once-fine maroon brocaded chairs and divans. Darlene didn't seem to notice the drabness. She was making plans. "We could re-upholster the furniture and have a beautiful place, Loren. I can just see kids here, relaxing between classes.

"And look in here!" she put Karen down to crawl around on the faded Oriental rug. A set of French doors led from the lobby into the main dining room. "This would be a perfect classroom." We climbed the wide staircase, exploring all five floors and all 32 rooms.

But it was when Darlene found "our" room that I knew she had already moved in. It was on a corner of the second floor and it had its own bathroom with a large European-style tub. French windows opened to catch the breeze and let in the music of cowbells.

"So you think this could be home for a while?" I asked smiling.

"Oh, yes!"

I walked through the hotel again imagining what could be done. The purpose of this school would not be to fill minds but to change lives: to increase faith in God and learn of His character and how our character could be like His. Here we would be bonded to the Lord and in the process, we'd be bonded to each other. Here we could learn about the twin nature of the gospel as I had glimpsed it back in Nassau during Hurricane Cleo. Here in this rank-smelling building (almost like a stable, I smiled to myself) would be born a school which would see hundreds of kids come to know God in depth and learn how to make Him known to others.

I stepped into the dining room. We'd have the kids for three months in this future classroom then staff and students would take to the road for six more months of training in the field. Together, we'd trust God to meet our needs. Together, we'd put into practice what had been learned in the classroom, talking to people about the Lord. "These young people will come back with their own visions," I said half aloud. "It'll multiply. . . ."

Dar came in. "Honey, the landlady wants to talk about terms."

"Good. Let's pray about this first." We stood there in the dining room, holding Karen between us and prayed. We believed God had brought us to this spot, and now we asked Him to bring to birth all we had been seeing for this very special school. As we prayed, my mind went to Kalafi Moala. I so much wished that he could attend this school. I was uneasy that Kalafi had not been trained, either as Dar and I had been trained, or in a school. Kalafi should be with us. He had married a Tongan girl named Tapu. Jimmy and Jannie knew her and reported that she was pretty. "*And* she's from one of the noble families of Tonga," Jannie added. "They're quite a team!" Still, I was uneasy. Kalafi had a lot of responsibility in his new missionary work in New Guinea for someone so young!

But for now my attention was focused on this school in Switzerland and all that was about to take place. We leased the hotel and we proceeded with plans for 36 young people from five nations to be with us, not quite realizing that we were also about to be launched into another one of the most basic lessons in guidance.

Ever since that breakthrough experience in the Dawsons' home in New Zealand, when I experienced such a deep surgery of the soul, I'd known that being transparently honest before God and before man was necessary if we were to make progress hearing God's voice. I'd seen for myself how God's power was released after a time of cleansing, and I remembered that in every great historical move of the Spirit which I had studied, there had been times of confession. I could see why, too. The cleansing season had set me free—the devil had none of my secret resentments and sins to hold over me anymore.

I'd never wanted to press confession with YWAMers but I

wondered if some day, others would experience it too. So what happened with my friend Don Stephens as we were getting started was no surprise.

It began December 27, 1969, six months after Dar and I first saw the Hotel Golf. The very next day classes would begin with our first visiting teacher. Don Stephens and his bride were with us. Don and Deyon had gotten married shortly after our launchpad experience in the Bahamas. That night I asked Don if he would speak to the group. He stood before us now, his sturdy frame more filled out than it had been in the Bahamas, and told us how God had called him to missions. It was in a small chapel in the mountains, he related, and he was kneeling at the front when he first received the impression that he was to be in full-time work overseas.

A few weeks later, after hearing a teaching session on the power of a clean conscience, I noticed that Don was squirming in his seat. Finally, he jumped to his feet.

"I have something to say. I exaggerated . . . no, I *lied* that first night we were here together when I told you guys how God called me. He did call me, the way I said . . . up to a point. But then I got carried away. I added some things that . . . weren't true. I lied. And I'm really sorry." Then he quickly sat down.

Don's honesty was being matched all over the room as others unburdened themselves. It was an amazing thing to watch. Not every person, of course, chose to confess aloud that night and that was all right too. Each could have confessed quietly to God alone. That, in fact, is the only confession that brings salvation. But confession to man brings humility and unity and makes a repentant person ready to receive God's healing of mind, emotion and body. Confession *is* good for the soul. We were seeing, before our very eyes, that there are special advantages in confessing to a loyal and supportive group. I noticed as we told our faults to one another we began to feel even closer, like a real family. At that moment, I could imagine myself being willing to die for Don, who had humbled himself. And for the others, too.[1]

---

1. Every individual has the right to confess his faults as the Holy Spirit convicts.

Later, when the students went to their rooms, they wrote letters making things right with parents, pastors, teachers and former sweethearts.

I remembered that little pile of letters on the desk in the Dawsons' basement room. And I remembered how, after that time of my own confession, the work of YWAM began to grow at a brand new and accelerated pace.

Would the same thing happen to Don?

At the end of the summer of 1970, Dar, Karen and I were walking in the forest by the hotel, talking about the school. I looked down at Dar, filling out with her second pregnancy, and thought that this day would tell us if our school idea really worked. Our 36 students had returned from their practical application trips all over Europe and as far away as Afghanistan, and soon we would hear their reports. As we strolled along through the pines, we looked forward to hearing the kids' stories—even though Dar and I had been able to visit personally a dozen of the locations in the previous weeks.

I wanted to to hear about their times on the field but I was even more eager to hear the students' future plans. Today was a big day because we would see the results of the guidance Darlene and I received together three-and-a-half years ago, confirmed by Willard Cantelon who received exactly the same word. Guidance, like prophecy, has one tough criterion for validity. Does it work?

Would this group of young people yield new ministries under the umbrella of YWAM? Today we would know, as the students gathered on the lawn outside the hotel. Today we would know.

Late that afternoon, with the Alps looking down on us, we were sitting in a circle of folding chairs in front of the hotel, under the arbor of sycamore trees. Dar was struggling with two-year-old Karen, who was being drawn like a magnet to Deyon's two-month-old-baby. Jimmy and Jannie were in the circle, just back

---

(James 5:16, I John 1, and David's example in II Samuel 11–12.) Two individuals have prayerfully volunteered their confessions in this book so that God's grace will be shown and others will be helped.

from Afghanistan, where they had led a small team. I looked at Jim and Jannie and wondered how much longer before their prayers were answered for a baby of their own after six years of marriage.

As we sat in the lacy shade of the trees, the 36 young people began to tell about their adventures in Germany, Spain, France, Great Britain, Yugoslavia, Bulgaria and Afghanistan. I filled everyone in on people who weren't able to be with us at this time—by this point we had inched up to forty staffers worldwide, including Kalafi and Tapu and their team in New Guinea.

Finally it was the time I had been waiting for—the time to hear the plans of those around the circle. It wasn't a disappointment. Person after person believed that God was telling him to stay on with YWAM in autonomous-yet-related missionary work in specialized areas of need. Was this really happening? Yes, we really were starting the multiplication process I'd dreamed of for so long . . . young people coming to us for short-term service, some staying on for our school then reaching out on their own to France, England, Germany, Spain. Jannie and Jimmy were going to Scandinavia.

I looked over at Don and Deyon Stephens for they were the only ones, sitting quietly at the end of the circle, who had as yet said nothing. Deyon's eyes were glittering, her broad smile even wider. "Don?" I asked. "What's up?"

Don sat forward in his chair and told how he had been so afraid I'd call on him that morning, because until lunch time he didn't know what he and Deyon were to do. They had been praying for weeks but nothing seemed clear.

"I had about given up. Nothing seemed to light a fire; we weren't getting any guidance. Then during lunch I picked up a new *Time* magazine from our bed. I opened it and started looking at the pictures of Munich, Germany, and the site they're building for the Summer Olympics two years from now in 1972. For some reason, I also remembered the thousands of communist youth I saw marching in East Berlin not long ago chanting slogans. It was eerie because none of those youths had any light in their eyes. They were like marching death."

He looked over to where I was sitting and drew a breath,

hitting his chest with his palm. "Loren," he said, "I believe we're supposed to have Christians marching in Munich during those Olympics! I think it would be a great opportunity to meet all kinds of people from both sides of the Iron Curtain and tell them about Jesus Christ. Why with all the athletes and visitors, it'll be like a world in miniature there!"

Something jumped inside me when he said it and I knew it was right. And I wasn't the only one—exclamations of excitement and approval were buzzing around the circle. Here was the idea of multiplication working at its best. YWAM was the catalyst for releasing people like Don. God had given this major idea to someone besides me in our little school. Remembering how Don had stood and humbled himself before the group, I was glad he was the one God had chosen. I trusted him.

"How many do you believe we should have there, Don?" I asked. He dropped his eyes a moment and said,

"Two hundred."

The number sounded low to me, but even at that it would be quite a feat. Especially in the light of the housing shortages that I knew would accompany the Olympics.

So that was our winding-up session. I had a tremendous sense of excitement about the event. Later we had a time of group prayer, sending people off with blessings in a dozen separate directions.

Finally Don and Deyon and their little one left too. They piled their Ford minibus high with gear and left us to scout out Munich.

I had a feeling we were on the verge of something very big.

Chapter Twelve

The Danger of Success

I wish with all my heart that I'd known—early enough to prevent the pain—one most important principle of guidance: *The Lord will lead us into victory, but success itself is the most dangerous obstacle to hearing properly the voice of God.*

We had no hint of this as we moved into the intertwining adventures that lay just ahead.

It was a raw, cold day two years after Don Stephens first glimpsed the dream of bringing volunteers to the Olympic Games. I was thinking about a giant Heidelberg press and worrying about where we were going to put it as I hustled down a gray sidewalk in Copenhagen. The press weighed two tons, and we wanted to use it to print a million pieces of literature for visitors to the Munich Olympics, just six months away. The press had been donated, along with money for paper and ink. Our only problem was that we had no place to put the huge press. It had to be delivered, set up and producing in two weeks.

I stepped off the curb, dodging a Volvo, and hunched down into my overcoat, anxious to get back to the warmth of Jimmy and Jannie's small, base-of-operations apartment.

Of course, a place to house a printing press was just a small part of our problem. We had hundreds of young people coming to Munich. Don admitted that he'd hedged when he first guessed we might have 200 volunteers. After recruiting in the U.S., Canada, South Africa and Europe, we now knew we would have closer to 1,000. And we still didn't have a place to put them!

Don had been to Munich several times looking for accommodations. On his first trip nearly two years ago, he learned that every large facility within a two hour drive of Munich had already been booked.

"At least we have to find a garage or something so we can get that press rolling!" had been the last decision as Don and I frantically searched for an answer to the immediate need.

I wasn't really worried about housing for the press or the kids either. Something would turn up, it always did. I thought back over the past two years and how easily things had been happening. We had found the formula and it was working! "It's all there, for any Christian to discover," I reminded myself perhaps a bit cockily. "Just get the word of the Lord on what He wants to do, declare His word aloud, and then watch it happen."

A year earlier, about one month before the birth of our son, David, God had spoken to us to buy the Hotel Golf. Up to this point all YWAM had owned was a few typewriters, a small used printing press (quite a step up from the old mimeograph we had used in the days when Bob and Lorraine were helping with our first newsletters!) and a meager collection of used vans and cars. But God had said buy, so we declared it. I set my mind and spirit never to doubt that the necessary money would be there, and on time.

Every week a little more arrived for the purchase of the Hotel Golf. We all did our part, too, the kids giving sacrifically with us for the purchase. Dar and I believed God was saying we should sell our "nest egg" house in La Puente and give that money. So we did. On the very last day the money was due, we were still lacking $10,000. I went by the post office to check our mail one last time before going to give our payment. There, waiting in our box were donations from several people who believed in what we were doing. I found it very hard to believe—the total was $10,060! Just out of curiosity, I watched the box for four days after we had paid the full amount, but nothing came in—not a dime.

I just knew that the housing in Munich would also work out. And we'd find a place to put the printing press. "But it had better be soon!" I thought, considering the Olympics were only six months away.

And sure enough, a few days later the phone rang. It was Don. "Loren, I think we've found a place for the printing press— and a thousand kids!"

"Yeah? That's great, what is it? A warehouse? A camp?"

"Well, no . . . it's a castle."

As he said the word castle, I heard that inner click. It was preposterous, but as Don described the castle that was for sale, I knew it was for us. When Don hung up I prayed about whether we were to buy the castle and began to grasp further vision that this facility was not just for the Olympics but for a permanent German base. Every hour the quiet "yes" inside me grew bigger.

A few days later I joined Don Stephens in Munich and together we went to look at the castle. We drove for an hour away from the city across flat farmland towards the village of Hurlach, turned down a country road and there it was—standing on the horizon like a giant. Our castle! It had twin towers with onion-shaped domes. Inching our way through the gates, around a circular drive, we pulled up to a massive, ornately-carved door and got out to crane our necks at the six-story castle and adjoining lower buildings.

"It's huge!" I whispered to Don.

We rang the bell and soon the *hausmeister* was leading us through the building. From dungeon to attic, everything was in mint condition. It had been built in the 16th century and the present owner, a children's social services group, had recently modernized the buildings at a cost twice the asking price! There were enough rooms and bathroom facilities for 300 people. But with various cavernous attics and two acres of grounds, I figured we could temporarily house many more hundreds.

"We said we needed a garage, and there it is," laughed Don. "It just came with a castle attached!" We walked briskly toward an adjacent building to see the garage—large enough for our Heidelberg press.

"And out back," I said, "we can put up a tent for a large training session."

We drove back to Munich with a German interpreter, walked

in to a meeting of the owners and made a proposal, using the detailed terms which I felt God had given me. We agreed to make a down payment within the week. Then we agreed to make another payment by the end of August—which would fall during our Olympics effort.

We came out a few minutes later with the keys to a castle. It was all so easy. Within one week, the money for the deposit came in from European Christian friends. Our faith was riding high. A few days later, the Heidelberg press was delivered to our castle at Hurlach, and our printers began to turn out gospel papers written in German, English and French.

At first it seemed the idea could not be from God:

It happened not long after Don moved into the castle, just four months before the games, in March of 1972. I was off on one more swing around the rim of the Pacific, urging young people to join us for the three-week effort in Munich. As I moved from country to country I really wasn't expecting what God did next, partly because His word had nothing to do with the Olympic Games. God was preparing us for events still distant.

I was flying from Seoul to Hong Kong and the stewardess had just removed my lunch tray. We were flying south above the Yellow Sea. I lifted the shade that covered the oblong porthole and there in the misty distance lay a body of land which I knew must be mainland China. We should be near Shanghai, I reckoned, somewhere in that distant haze.

Suddenly, God's voice cut into my thoughts. "It's time for you to pursue the ship."

I was astonished. "Is this You, God?" was my automatic question. Ever since Hurricane Cleo in the Bahamas, I'd realized that we were to have a twin nature to our mission—loving God and helping people. And a ship would be a perfect tool for both. But the thought overwhelmed me. I could just imagine all that a ship would entail, finding skilled crew, satisfying international shipping requirements, raising the enormous amount of money to keep a mercy ship afloat and provisioned.

"God, if You're saying now is the time to begin, please help

93

me to be certain. Taking on something this big would cost us dearly."

I had no idea how high the price would be.

A few weeks later in New Zealand I had just finished speaking to young people about Munich. I enjoyed coming back to this lovely country with its green, sheep-dotted hills. Here I had learned so many of the ways of God. I had met Kalafi Moala, Jim and Joy Dawson and others who meant so much to me. Now we had a fine core of leaders for YWAM New Zealand. I told these men about the experience in the Bahamas, and again in the airplane over Shanghai. Was God leading us toward a ship?

Six of us gathered to pray. "Lord, we need Your help. You know how hard it would be just to gather the right people . . ." someone was saying. Suddenly there was a knock at the door. Mildly annoyed at the interruption, I went to see who it was. There stood a weathered man of about 30.

"What is it, sir?" I asked, glancing over my shoulder at my friends who were waiting.

The man must have seen that he was interrupting for he blurted out: "Why would God call a man to missions when he's just not qualified?"

It was an odd question. But a nudge in my spirit told me to listen carefully. "Come in, won't you?" I opened the door wide. "What do you mean, unqualified?"

"I mean," the man said, stepping uneasily into the room, "all I know is the sea. I've been a chief engineer and a skipper, and yet I know God is calling me to missions! They never go together, do they?"

Well, of course we were overwhelmed at the direct way the Lord was answering us. The seaman, it turned out, wanted work right away which we couldn't supply. Nevertheless his coming by while we were praying for guidance caused a flurry of excitement. The first order of business was Munich, but now we knew that God was giving us marching orders for tomorrow.

I headed home, anxious to fill Dar in on what had happened and to catch up on Munich. I wouldn't have time to go by New Guinea to see Kalafi, Tapu and their two little girls. They had 25 staff members, but I reassured myself that Kalafi was probably doing a great job.

Dar and I and our children, aged four and eighteen months turned off the highway from Munich, through the flat farmland towards the castle. In just one week, hundreds of young people would be coming from literally every continent to this village. The sleepy hamlet with its half-timbered cottages, its pristine white Catholic church and handful of shops was in for a booming three weeks. Kids with backpacks were already walking through the village. "Do you realize, Dar," I said, turning our car toward the castle, "there are only a thousand residents in Hurlach? We'll double the population in just one week."

Dar laughed. "Yes, and do you realize, Loren Cunningham, that ten years ago you told me your life goal was to see a thousand young people in evangelism? Here they are!"

It was an interesting but not a satisfying remark. We now had goals way past that. Goals of twin ministries that were already in embryo.

I pulled up the circular drive and stopped in front of the massive carved front door. Don must have been waiting. He bounded out to greet us, followed by Deyon with their two-year-old blond doll. "Come back behind the castle, you guys. We have a surprise for you!"

There, just barely squeezed into the space between the castle and the back fence was a large, striped circus tent! Don told me how he had almost given up finding one since it seemed every big tent in Europe had been rented. But then a dance was canceled, ". . . and so we have our meeting place," Don said.

Chapter Thirteen

Munich: The World in Miniature

All that week the kids came in. A thousand of them. From 52 nations and representing 50 denominations. Jimmy and Jannie arrived in a VW camper. Jim and Joy Dawson were there—Jim, ever the elegant one and straight-talking Joy who would be one of the Bible teachers in our tent.

The plan for the three weeks was a simple one. Each day 500 young people under Don Stephens' leadership, would be on the streets of Munich while the other 500, under my leadership, would stay back at the castle getting replenished with lots of teaching, prayer and Bible reading. Then the following day the groups would trade places. The kids would get up at five in the morning, take sack lunches on the train to Munich, not returning until midnight. We hoped to have marches in the city and toward the end of the three weeks, a mammoth music festival.

From the very first day of the campaign, however, we met the worst kind of resistance we could imagine—*indifference*.

We were like uninvited guests at someone's party. The atmosphere in Munich was carnival. It was a tough assignment attempting to interrupt festivities to talk to people about weighty things. Sports was the giant idol—it had the world at its feet. Athletic competition was the answer to peace and brotherhood. The German authorities, anxious to have a smooth-running Olympics to show the world, forbade the marches we had planned and put us outside Munich for our music.

So we had to improvise. We specialized in small teams, some going onto school campuses, into parks where young communists and spaced-out street people congregated, holding impromptu rallies throughout the city and on the Olympic grounds. In the Athletes' Village our kids talked to participants from behind the Iron Curtain. When we found someone who wanted to learn more, we brought him to a large store we'd turned into a coffeehouse. There we talked about Jesus.

We were getting fair results but the going was rough. We'd been at work for two weeks and the big problem in this atmosphere of fun and competition was still the shrug-of-shoulder indifference.

All of this changed when the idol of world-brotherhood-through-sports cracked and fell.

I was speaking in the big striped tent early Tuesday morning, September 5, when I noticed unrest near the back. Whispers were passing down the rows of seats, faces darkening with worry. Finally, a denim-clad volunteer hustled up the dirt aisle and handed me a note.

I read it in disbelief. Arab terrorists had broken into the Athletes' Village, killing two Israeli contestants and taking nine hostage. I announced the news to the young people and we began to pray.

We suspended classes, broke into small groups and asked God somehow in some way to bring good out of this tragedy. We learned later that the 500 YWAMers who were in the city with Don were doing the same thing wherever they were. They knelt in silent circles yards away from the police-cordoned area where the terrorists held the athletes hostage. Other YWAMers knelt on the sidewalks of downtown Munich. They knelt at our coffeehouse. And we held our breath together with the rest of the world.

Swiftly, in an explosion of violence, the drama ended and nine more Israelis, five Arabs and one German were killed.

Overnight the carnival of the Olympics turned into a funeral. People milled about in the streets, lost. Suddenly our young people were accepted, for we were in Munich as emissaries of hope. We wept with the weeping, assuring them that Jesus Christ held the answer to tragedies like this. And hearts were open: On the very day of the terrorist attack a young Israeli YWAM girl led an Arab Moslem to faith in her Messiah.

Dar and I could no longer stay out in the country. We had to go into Munich with the rest of our young people. We stood with a group in the entertainment area of the Olympic grounds, singing and directing attention to God. One by one, people filled the amphitheater, quietly listening to us. As we finished an attractive German girl, about twenty came up to us and asked, "You are a Jesus People?"

Dar and I answered at the same time. "Yes." A look of intense longing came over the German girl.

"I'm not a Jesus People. But I want to be." We took her to the coffeehouse and introduced her to Don, who was fluent in German. He found out she had been wandering through Europe, trying to find meaning to life. She found it that night, announcing with a sweep of her arm, "Now I know Jesus. I am a Jesus People too!"

After the Israeli athletes' tragedy, city officials changed their minds about us. One police officer told Don, "You Christians are the only good that has happened here in the last three weeks." They now allowed us to march, even donating thousands of flowers from city gardens for us to give out as we walked through the heart of the city, a thousand strong, in sympathy for the slain. We printed 10,000 newspapers on our Heidelberg press out in the castle garage.

The papers were grabbed out of our hands.

They featured a picture of an Arab YWAMer and a Jewish YWAMer standing arm in arm, proclaiming that the only answer for world brotherhood was Jesus Christ.

The three weeks at the Olympics were over, having ended in a tragic drama which Munich would never forget. The three weeks were over for us, too. They'd allowed participation in people's sorrow but we sensed they also marked a new beginning. Through generous gifts we met the payment on our castle and knew that we now had a permanent anchor place in Germany. Just before the big striped tent came down we had an offering where our young people could either put money *into* the basket or take *from* the basket, depending on their guidance and next plans. Many of the volunteers needed air fare because they had chosen to go on to one of our twenty center's throughout the world and continue working with YWAM. Others chose to go to one of the three schools that had sprung up after our Lausanne prototype. In almost every case there was an added expense: the long trans-Atlantic or trans-Pacific phone calls back home to discuss new plans with mothers and fathers, because we stressed keeping lines of communication open with parents and churches.

The end of the Olympics allowed me to shift my attention, too. The next place where I needed special guidance was the ship. I somehow knew just what the ship would be like: about 500 feet long, able to sleep several hundred, a floating campus for a school and large cargo holds able to carry materials to needy people. We'd have medical teams aboard and hundreds of young people to off-load at ports carrying the Good News. We would paint the ship white—symbolizing the purity of God.

When the third individual told me about an inter-island ferry named the *Maori* for sale in New Zealand, I began to take notice.

In April of 1973, thirteen months after God told me to pursue the ship, I headed for New Zealand to take a look at the *Maori*. Already, we had found a captain and other qualified crew members; even now they were in Lausanne, going through our school.

Flying into Wellington, my plane made its final approach low over the harbor. The hilly city, wrapped around a bay, looked much like San Francisco.

Then, below me, I saw her. She could only be the *Maori*. She was just as friends had described her, a black ship about 450 feet long with white upper decks and an orange and blue funnel, sitting squarely confident at the foot of Wellington's hills. I thought with assurance, "I am looking down on our destiny!"

A representative from the Union Steamship Company and one of our directors from YWAM-New Zealand were with me as I climbed the gangplank onto the *Maori*. It really was a fine vessel. Three decks above, two decks below, sleeping 920 with a large car deck that would accommodate 120 vehicles or tons of cargo. There was a restaurant and lounge and a small infirmary. I just knew, without even a second thought, that this was the ship we'd been waiting for. We drove away, leaving the *Maori* sitting, proudly, at her mooring.

I didn't have a hint, not one—as we got go-ahead signals from many directions—that I was stepping into the saddest mistake we can make in seeking to hear God's voice. It is a mistake, ironically, that comes late in an adventure in guidance, right at the time when everything is going very well indeed.

Chapter Fourteen

The Man in the Shadows

I was really not all that interested in money—Dar and I and five-year-old Karen and two-year-old David still lived in four rooms in an annex of the Lausanne Hotel. I was, however, very interested in the *guidance* aspect of money and it seemed we were rapidly being led to purchase the *Maori*. Four months after seeing the ship myself, I sent Wally Wenge, my administrative assistant, to New Zealand to negotiate with the Union Steamship Company for the vessel. We agreed to give a deposit of $72,000, by September 4, 1973. The rest would be due in thirty days.

Right away we were encouraged. A businessman called me from England saying that God was telling him to do something for YWAM. The amount he sent was more than enough for our deposit. Wally Wenge phoned to say that stories were appearing in the New Zealand press about some young missionaries claiming God told them to buy the *Maori*! The ship had been in service for a long time in New Zealand and she had become something of a landmark. People were interested in our story. Soon everyone in the country knew about our deal.

We felt confident. Given the success we'd had in the past, that confidence seemed justified. We made some added statements to the press stressing the fact that God not only speaks to His people, He also provides. The papers loved it. One headline read, "Youth Say 'God Will Give Us The Ship!' " We announced that the ship would be sailing from New Zealand to California in thirty days, when the balance of our payment was due. She would arrive there mid-October—two months from now. I was riding high. And why not? Every day, we saw some new release. Either it would be a volunteer or money or a special offer: one company promised free paint to re-do the *Maori* all in white; the interior decorator of the *Queen Elizabeth II* volunteered his services free of charge; some farmers promised grains and meat to take to the needy. Most importantly, a businessman from Manila promised the remainder of the purchase price. All he needed to do was get his funds out of the Philippines.

Things were happening fast.

Simply administering these releases kept me spinning. One day, I began to feel the need to slow down. In fact I needed a week alone with God, fasting and praying.

In that week everything changed.

I was sitting quietly, praying, with my Bible open to Hebrews. Suddenly the words of chapter 12, verses 26 and 27 leaped off the page. *"Yet once more I shake not the earth only, but also heaven . . . that those things which cannot be shaken may remain"* (italics added).

A rock hit the bottom of my stomach. "Oh, no! I hope that doesn't mean the ship!"

The next day, with no little anxiety, I called our California office where Jim Dawson was now the administrator after he and Joy had joined us as full-timers.

"What came in for the ship today?" I asked.

"Not a thing, Loren." Odd.

"Has our Manila businessman gotten his money out of the Philippines yet?"

There was no news from the Philippines. Odd. We all thought that was going to be routine. I was puzzled. The words on that page of Hebrews had had such power in them! Maybe they *did* mean the ship!

For the rest of my week of prayer I struggled with this apparent warning-guidance, but nothing became clear. Perhaps I'd learn more when I met with 93 of our YWAM leaders, next week, in Osaka, Japan. We had good experience hearing God when we were all together.

Two weeks before our deadline for paying the Union Steamship Company I kissed Darlene goodby and set out for Osaka via, (as it turned out) an important stopover in Seoul, Korea.

On my way I thought about how crucial these yearly leadership gatherings had become. In the thirteen years since our beginning we had grown into a family of 200 individual missionaries from 15 countries, each running a separate base with local funding and autonomy. We were linked in our friendship and in spirit by common call and vision. With such decentralization, YWAM depended on meetings like this upcoming one in Osaka. Our relationship to each other was the glue holding us together.

Which made my position all the more difficult if that word from God about "shakings" did concern the ship. I cringed at the thought of facing my friends (Don Stephens would be there and Jim and Joy Dawson, my sister Jannie and her husband, Jim, Kalafi and his wife, Tapu . . . scores of others) and telling them the ship was in jeopardy.

As the air miles passed I began to think perhaps the warning I'd received in Hebrews did not refer to our ship. Bit by bit my confidence returned. When I got to the stopover in Seoul I phoned my assistant, Wally Wenge, in New Zealand. He was very positive. Our 110 volunteers and crew members from ten nations were hard at work cleaning the ship and polishing it from stem to stern. Good!

The mood of confidence was the reason, I am certain, for my being so shattered by the strange event which followed.

Early the next morning, I was lying on the floor atop my Asian pallet bed, praying. In three days I would be flying to Osaka for the conference. The deadline for the ship money was now ten days away.

I gradually quieted my mind, centering down on Jesus, yielding to Him and worshiping him, ready to listen to anything His Spirit wanted to say in my mind.

Suddenly I was looking at a mental picture. It was not unlike the picture of the waves I'd seen 17 years ago. Only this time, the vision was terrifying. . . .

I saw myself standing before a crowd of YWAM leaders. I announced with exuberance, "We've got the ship! God has given us the money for the *Maori*!" The crowd cheered wildly, waving arms and shouting. Then all of a sudden I saw a figure standing in the shadows to my left, unnoticed by any of us. I looked closer at his face and saw that he was grieving. Then it hit me—this was Jesus! We were ignoring Him! We were cheering a ship and forgetting Jesus!

I buried my face in the pallet bed, unable to wipe away the horrible sight. "Oh, God! Forgive me! I have gotten my eyes on the ship You're giving us and have taken them off You! I . . . we . . . do not deserve to have it! We don't want to rob You of Your glory and give it to a hunk of metal."

I cried a long time and felt that God had heard and forgiven me. But I knew my attitude wasn't the only one which needed correcting. I had a somber message to give the leaders on Monday in Osaka. We had to do some serious business with the Lord before we thought about anything else.

It was all I could do to force a smile as we deplaned at the Osaka airport. Kalafi's work with YWAM was located there in Japan and it was he and his wife, Tapu, who met me. Kalafi hadn't changed, except that his square frame was filling out some. "You're looking more like a royal Tongan," I said, trying not to let my grief show for now. Kalafi's wife was shorter than he was, pretty, with black, soft curly hair and a shy smile. They began to bustle me towards their van, warning me about the rustic hostel they had found for our meetings. "It's not the Ritz," Kalafi said.

We chatted about their work as we drove. Was it my imagination, or did Kalafi seem less lighthearted than I remembered? Maybe it was the years . . . he had been a slender eighteen-year-old when I first met him in New Zealand six years ago. Kalafi answered my questions, telling me enthusiastically all about their work with the university students. I dismissed my first impressions.

Kalafi parked in front of the two-story, spartan hostel in Otsu City, outside of Osaka. All my YWAM friends rushed up to greet me, as we entered the terrazzo-floored lobby. The mood of every man and woman was upbeat, and I quietly nursed my dark secret.

I was issued hard plastic slippers, a towel and sheets by an efficient Japanese matron, then climbed the stone steps to my room. I threw the sheets onto a bunk and lay down. I didn't look forward to our first meeting that afternoon.

On the second floor was a conference room where three semi-circular rows of chairs waited for us. We settled into our places. "There won't be much to distract us," I thought, looking at the bare room.

I stood up and every eye riveted on me expecting, I knew, to hear the latest good news about the ship.

I spoke instead about the vision God had given me—of Jesus grieving in the shadows while we praised a hunk of metal.

It was a simple story, really. Yes, God had told us to get a ship, and repeatedly He had confirmed His guidance, using all the ways we had learned for hearing His voice. He used the Wise Men Principle; He used Scriptures which He seemed to lift off the pages for us; He used provision of money and people, and that inner conviction—but we had failed in the *way* we had carried out His guidance. We had subtly turned from the Giver to the gift.

The reaction of everyone was immediate and almost unanimous . . . and it was the same as my own when I was alone on my Asian pallet bed in Seoul. Some fell to their knees or to their very faces. Someone began to cry. Soon we were weeping, strong men and women, crying.

For six days, we came together not to rejoice because we had a ship but to confess places in our lives where we had failed to put God first or had robbed Him of His glory. The confessions continued day after day. Kalafi was one who spoke up. He stood, his face grave, and mentioned briefly that he was having trouble in his marriage. Kalafi and Tapu were in trouble? I asked myself, surprised. Kalafi didn't elaborate, and somehow with the weight of all that was being unearthed, I didn't get around to finding him alone to see if I could help.

Every day we came into the bare, austere meeting room, expecting the heavy feeling of guilt to lift. Every day we found new areas which needed purifying. A painful awareness of God's awesome holiness coursed through the room. We began to sense great corporate shortcomings. The big one was pride. To our horror we saw that we'd begun to think that Youth With A Mission was God's "favorite tool": we were "the most spiritual" mission; we had learned "more about faith" than others; we had "a corner on releases." We saw down into our hearts and it was disgusting. For the first time, I glimpsed something of what it will be like to stand before God in Judgment.

There was nothing to do but throw ourselves on His mercy. On the seventh day we were singing softly when suddenly a special, deep quietness settled over us. Through some instinct of the spirit, we knew He had walked into that bare conference room on the second floor of a hostel outside Osaka. He removed all the guilt. We were clean, forgiven.

After a time of rejoicing I kept thinking He would say something about the ship. But it didn't happen. I did not know what to do. I could only hope that our repentance had been in time, and that somehow, with right priorities and by keeping our eyes on Him instead of on a tool, He would heal this situation and still give us the ship.

But no such healing came to us. The deadline for closing on the *Maori* arrived. I called Wally in New Zealand and told him what had been happening. He was, of course, as stunned as we were. I asked him to see if he could get an extension from the Union Steamship Company. Wally called back to say we'd been granted four weeks. But the crew, he said, had to move off the ship and stop the renovations. About half were going home, but sixty were staying and were being housed by Christians in Wellington.

"What about a loan, Loren?" Wally ventured. "Three people have offered to lend us money to buy the ship." His voice lacked conviction and we both knew that accepting a loan at this time wouldn't be right.

We left Osaka limping, saying our goodbyes, going back to our individual duty posts around the world. I headed back to Dar who had flown to California from Switzerland and was waiting, as numbed as all of us at the new developments. She and I had expected to be in California when the *Maori* sailed in.

Now, back in the States, Darlene and I settled down to some long prayer times. "Is this really You, Lord?" I found myself saying over and over again. Why had God not healed our ship ministry? Perhaps He would still do so in the three weeks before the new deadline on November 2. "Help us, dear Lord, help us to understand what You're doing." Darlene prayed.

That prayer, at least, was answered. The insight came through one of the people who had been at the Osaka conference, Joy Dawson, who telephoned a few days later.

"Loren," Joy said, "I have just finished reading the story of Lazarus. I was reading the part where Jesus chose not to *heal* Lazarus. He waited instead until His friend died, then *resurrected* him. In this case, a resurrection brought more glory to God than a healing."

My chest tightened. "Loren, I believe God is saying this to YWAM right now—that He is giving us a choice. We can have a healing of the ship. But greater glory will come to Him if we accept a resurrection. The hard part is that if we let the ship die, something of us will die right along with it . . . our 'reputation.' As for me and my little part in YWAM, I'd prefer the latter."

The certainty that Joy was speaking truth blocked out everything else. I knew the choice that was before me now. After we hung up I prayed by myself to make sure, but the truth only grew larger in my mind. God was giving us a chance to give greater honor to Him by letting our dream die so that He could resurrect it.

First, of course, plans for the *Maori* did have to die. Really die. And we had to "die" right along with them. Remembering all that had been written about us in the New Zealand papers, especially those times when we said flatly that God would give us a ship, I knew I had to make something right with the people in New Zealand. People's trust in God may have been hurt. People would easily doubt that He speaks and provides.

I sat down and wrote a letter to a newspaper of New Zealand. The letter was printed, telling how God had guided us to buy a ship, but *we* had failed by giving greater honor to the ship than to the Lord. The response was immediate and hostile, especially among some Christians who saw us as having made presumptuous claims. What could I say! All I knew was that ever since the day, four weeks ago, when I read in Hebrews that God was going to shake what could be shaken, not one dollar had come in for the ship, (in total contrast to the last six months) not one item pledged, not one additional worker or service released. Nothing. And still the Philippine government refused to budge regarding our friend's personal funds. This had all happened even though there was no way for people to have known of any change. Suddenly the flow had been turned off and only God could have done it.

The gracious gentlemen of the Union Steamship Company again gave us an extension—one week this time. We accepted, because we had no idea what shape God's resurrection would take. But the end seemed near. It was like watching a loved one wasting away with terrible disease.

To make matters even worse we still had ninety students coming to our team houses in L.A. ready to join the ship for an on-board school. I made the necessary calls and gave them the choice of meeting us for a school in Hawaii instead.

I must say that my heart was heavy when I flew out of L.A. International Airport a few weeks later with my family, heading for Hawaii. Then, as we drove over Pali Highway from the Honolulu Airport, I reflected on how different our visit was this time. The sunshine was the same, the brilliant blue water surrounding Diamond Head was the same. Nothing was different about the plumeria trees with their yellow, white and pink flowers. No, the difference was inside. The times I had come to Hawaii before had been joyful expectation—trying a brand new experiment, rejoining Darlene after a long absence, planning a school that was different from anything we had ever seen.

This time we were coming to Hawaii to wait.

We pulled off the highway into a camp in Kaneohe, on the other side of the island from Honolulu. Beside the parking lot, facing Kaneohe Bay, was the dining room/meeting hall and kitchen. On the parking lot was a pay phone—not a booth, just a plastic bubble on a pole protecting the phone. It was the only phone available in the camp. I knew I'd be spending a lot of time in front of that bubble as we groped our way through the morass of the *Maori*.

Darlene and I and the children made our way to the cabins;

wooden structures with walls only two-thirds of the way up the sides and topped with screens. There were no closets and no plumbing: the bathrooms were in separate buildings. It was just a camp.

But it was in this rustic setting that we received the most startling of guidance experiences to date.

Chapter Fifteen

Three Steps to Hearing God

There was no hint of guidance in the early stages of this next unfolding of God's plan for our lives. It seemed we were only waiting. The ship was dead. Our "reputations" were bruised. But the thing that made Dar and me most uncomfortable was the lack of clear direction.

"But are we being obedient, Loren?" Dar asked as I groused around, unpacking. Well, yes. I did think we were being obedient. "Then let's just listen. God will show us what He's doing!"

Dar busied herself making a home out of our tiny cabin at Kaneohe. There was barely room for two sets of bunks. Dar strung up a clothesline marking out a closet, put my briefcase on the floor and announced that it was my office. And of course Dar brought out Karen's and David's own bowls and cups and their pictures of grandparents, aunts, uncles and cousins. It wasn't too different from the tent-house, with boxes for furniture, that my folks had in Somerton, Arizona.

Virtually all of the 92 students showed up! I was astonished at the wonderful flexibility of youth. Jim and Jan Rogers came out too. When we all gathered in the camp dining room and I explained what was happening, everyone joined in, praying for guidance and waiting expectantly. I spent lots of time at the bubble-topped phone in the parking lot, talking to Wally Wenge in New Zealand about the *Maori*. The Union Steamship Company was extending the deadline one day at a time now. Then the November winds and rains started, blowing in through our screen-topped bungalows. Soon we were locked in a mire of mud at our camp. When I asked God if we were doing what He wanted us to do He just said yes, the waiting wouldn't last forever. More days passed and I could still see no direction.

The breakthrough started one amazing night. I had decided to stay up all night and pray, asking three of the school staff, Jimmy and Jannie and Reona Peterson to join me. Dar felt she was to stay with the children. The four of us walked to a small, wooden annex about 10:00 p.m., turned on the light and went in. We knelt down on the rough floor beside some folding chairs. We followed the Three Steps to Hearing God which I had first learned from Joy Dawson in New Zealand. First we took Christ's authority to silence the enemy. Second, we asked the Lord to clear from our minds any presumptions and preconceived ideas. Third, we waited . . . believing He would speak in the way and in the time which He chose.

A cool breeze stirred in from the bay and gecko lizards chirped on the walls as we waited for God to speak in our minds.

We had a spirited time of praying for the ship ministry then we waited again. The pointed black hands on the big wall clock read 11:00 p.m. Reona said a Scripture reference had come into her mind. Luke 4:4. I remembered the time I'd initially met this kind of guidance, on my first visit to New Zealand. People would "hear" a Scripture reference in their minds, without knowing what the verse said. The key, we were taught there, was yielded-ness to Jesus. We weren't playing some kind of game, pulling a reference out of the air; we were waiting, listening, focusing our minds on Jesus alone. Then, if He told us to look up a particular verse we did so, knowing that God could use whatever means He chose to guide His people. Now, in that all-night prayer session when we looked up the reference Reona had heard we found a verse encouraging us to continue listening for God's voice—the passage in Luke where Jesus said that man lives by every word that comes from God.

Again we returned to silence. The hands of the clock swept to 1:30 a.m., but an air of anticipation kept me alert. I knew God was about to speak. There was another long time of silent seeking.

It was surprising to see that the clock said 3:30. And I saw that my poor sister had fallen asleep kneeling at her chair.

Then, suddenly the three of us began quickly to get words from God. Two things came hard into my mind. One was the word "Kona." I knew that was a place on the Big Island, though I'd never been there. The second was a mental picture of a lighthouse on the Big Island with rays beaming across the Pacific towards Asia.

I didn't understand. The question on my mind was a resurrected ship ministry. Yet God was saying Kona and a lighthouse. I broke the silence and told Reona and Jimmy this impression (Jannie was still asleep), then suggested we go back to God for "Round Two." "Lord," I prayed, "help us understand what you are saying."

More thoughts came to us. The idea of some kind of school that was not another of our regular Schools of Evangelism, but much broader in its training. Reona heard God speak about a farm, of all things. And the biggest puzzle of all, the picture came of a big white ship in a bay.

The black hands now read 5:30 in the morning. My mind was reeling with all this brand new information. A lighthouse. A large school. The Big Island—Kona. A farm. A white ship in a bay.

Jimmy woke Jannie and we stood up stiffly. I thanked the others for joining me and went down the dark, muddy path to our cabin. I crawled into my bunk and sank into sleep, exhausted yet exhilarated.

It seemed only minutes until Dar was shaking my shoulder gently, telling me it was time to wake up. I hurriedly told her about the incredible night then hurried to the dining room for the morning school session. The students were already sitting at the long tables which had been wiped clean from breakfast. Ninety faces looked up at me. Most were young people, girls with long straight hair parted in the middle, wearing jeans or granny skirts. The fellows were uniformly in jeans, some with long hair and beards, others clean-shaven.

"A few of us just spent a very interesting night hearing from the Lord," I began. "But I don't know if God wants me to tell you what He said. So we'll wait to see if He says any of the same things to you." I ran through the same steps for listening to the Lord which we had used: take authority over the enemy, clear away your own preconceived ideas, then listen for Jesus' voice.

Then we waited.

Shouts of children filtered in from the playground next door.

"Who wants to be first?"

Shyly, a moon-faced girl with round, rimless glasses spoke. "This sounds funny, but I just get this impression of a big letter 'K.'"

Strange, I thought. "Anyone else?"

A guy with a blond beard quickly spoke, "I got the word 'Kona!'" Now I was getting excited. Someone else got "volcano." The only active volcanoes in Hawaii were on the Big Island.

The incredible morning went on, the kids popping up with words from God all over the room. "I see a picture of a big place—I think it's some kind of school," one boy said. Someone else mentioned a farm, and someone saw a white house on a hill.

My pulse was pounding with excitement. So much was being repeated from last night that, frankly, I had trouble *believing* what I heard. I was glad there were 90 people there who could be witnesses.

The part that really stirred me came right at the end of the seeking session.

One girl saw a ship.

She said it was white and it lay at anchor in the bay of an island.

What on earth had been happening! Two weeks passed after that incredible all-night seeking experience. We had had an amazing glimpse into the future. But now I had to come to grips with present realities . . . the death of a ship, and sixty crew members who I knew had been wounded. So in early December I went to New Zealand. Wally Wenge met me at the Wellington airport. His face was gray. "There's no point waiting to tell you, good friend. It's official—the Union Steamship Company has just closed the negotiations. We've lost our ship."

Neither of us said much as Wally drove me to the harbor to see our deceased dream. December was early summer in the

Southern Hemisphere and the sun sparkled on the bay, a scene that did not match our moods. Wally and I stood in front of the *Maori,* tied to the dock with its gangplank up, forbidding entrance. I suddenly realized that we were both silent, as if before a casket.

Then we went to see the sixty remnant crew members. I told them about Lazarus. "If we're right in our guidance, the *Maori* is not going to 'be healed' for us. She is now dead and the Lord will resurrect the dream in whatever fashion He chooses."

Looking out over their faces—men, women, teenagers who had given so much—I could feel the hurt. Some had come to New Zealand from far away for the dream. Many had given up good positions, sacrificing salaries, promotions. Together they had spent thousands of hours cleaning and scrubbing the *Maori,* putting love into the sudsy water on her decks. It hurt them the most.

When I got back to Hawaii, I knew someone who had to be told about the end of our dream. It was raining again and I huddled under an umbrella as I stood at my pay phone in the parking lot of the Kaneohe camp. I gave the operator the number I wanted: the residence of the man in England who had given us the money for the ship deposit. The deposit we had just forfeited. Miserably, I hunched under my umbrella as the phone rang on the other end of the line. I felt a little like I'd felt when I was ten and had lost Mom's five-dollar grocery money.

The clipped, British voice answered and I plunged in. I explained what had happened including the grieving Jesus and the Osaka confessions of our sins, especially our pride; I told him how confession opened the door to His guidance again and that God had given us a choice: we could either "heal" this situation with the *Maori* or take a harder road and trust Him for a resurrection of our dream in whatever manner He chose.

"What you're trying to say, Loren, is that you've lost the deposit money," my friend said.

"That's . . . that's right."

The only sound coming over my bubble-topped phone at Kaneohe was the crackle of the cable connection. Finally my

British friend spoke. "I consider my money well invested, Loren! God has used it to get your organization humbled before Him. I expect you to move ahead with a special power now. Congratulations!"

Now I was *really* humbled. What a man of God this English businessman was!

It was dawn in Kaneohe, Hawaii, but I was already awake. A month had passed since we lost the ship. Dar and I, Karen and David lay on our bunks in our screened cabin. Our suitcases were packed, waiting by the door. We were going home to Switzerland.

Lying there in the dawn light, I thought back over the past ten weeks of school. Those weeks were to have been on our ship. We held classes instead in a muddy camp. I was amazed at how well the young people adapted—not just to the physical miseries, but to the uncertainties. And now it was time to go home to Switzerland.

Home. It was a little perplexing, for something told me I'd be back here someday. Despite all the wind, rain and mud, I had felt roots going down. Especially since that amazing all-night seeking session, followed in the morning with the kids having the same strange guidance which, so far at least, nobody fully understood.

Our plane settled into the wintry valley by Lake Geneva. Don Stephens met us, his straight brown hair all but covered with a Russian-style fur hat. Don drove us home to the Lausanne hotel. The familiar square building looked welcoming by its evergreen forest. The hotel was now painted beige; the old peeling green shutters were freshly done in chocolate brown. We stood for a moment in the parking lot, our breath hanging in clouds, and remembered how we had first seen this building all boarded up more than four years earlier. We'd moved in with dreams and little else and began to clean out the cobwebs. Since then almost all of those dreams had come true. We'd sent out thousands of workers to 60 countries, acquiring bases of operation in 35 locations.

Just one very important dream had not come true. The ship.

Don was dragging our suitcases out of his car, so I hurried to join him. When we reached our apartment in the hotel annex, David, aged three, plumped his teddy bear on his bed across from his five-year-old sister's and we were home.

Except somehow I didn't feel like it.

Could that very reaction be a part of what God was saying to us? Over the next weeks as we settled into the familiar routine I had trouble focusing my mind. One morning during a class I tried to analyze my discontent. Don had done a great job in my absence. Reports came in from all over Europe about the creative, innovative evangelism of the kids under his leadership.

Don was now talking to the kids in the classroom about plans for the summer. Suddenly, I saw him look toward me, uncertainly. I could read his mind. Perhaps he should be checking with me first? The moment passed and Don went on talking, but not before I realized the multiplication had really taken place. Don was the leader at this base now. It was time to move on to new adventures of my own.

It was a strange time for someone interested in guidance because although I was clearly being led *away* from one area I was not as clearly being led *to* another. I wasn't supposed to stay in Europe, that seemed certain. And the ship was gone. We had lost her, irretrievably.

One day while I was sitting in my favorite chair, a rocker, in our annex apartment, Wally Wenge called from New Zealand.

"Loren, I thought you'd want to know . . . the *Maori* was towed out to sea today. She's been sold for scrap to a Taiwan salvage company. Some of our crew stood on the dock and watched the tug pull her away. . . ."

I hung up and looked out on the fog-shrouded mountains, feeling the same helplessness I felt when Aunt Sandra and later, Aunt Arnette died of cancer. The happy chatter of Karen and David drifted in from their room. Dar came in with mugs of steaming cocoa. I told her about Wally's phone call.

"The *Maori* is dead—dead, Darlene." She didn't say anything. We just sat there, looking out the window at the January mist. I thought about the pain that had followed in the four months since God said He was going to shake what could be shaken. "I've never felt so . . . without direction. . . ."

"I know, sweetheart. We've lost our axehead."

I knew immediately what guidance principle Darlene was referring to. Duncan Campbell, who taught for three years at our schools, told us about Elisha and his school of the prophets. One of Elisha's students lost the head off his axe. Elisha instructed the young man to go back to the place where he last knew he had it. There, at that spot, God again gave him the tool he needed. Sometimes, Duncan said, we momentarily lose our axeheads— our best cutting-edge tool for ministry, the clear voice of God. It helps to go back to the place where we last knew we had heard the sharp edge of God's voice.

Where was the last place that we knew God was speaking to us?

I saw it very clearly.

"There's no doubt, Dar," I said. "The last place we had our axehead was at that all-night prayer meeting in Hawaii." And what had He said? We had gone into that night asking God about the *Maori* but instead He talked to us about a lighthouse for the Pacific and Asia on the Big Island.

Dar and I talked late into the afternoon—our cocoa growing cold and forgotten on the table beside us—as we remembered the words God had given so mysteriously to separate groups. He had spoken about the Kona coast of the Big Island, about a big white house on a hill, about a farm, a new kind of school . . . even about a white ship in a bay. Surely, that was where the axehead lay.

We found ourselves particularly intrigued by the idea of the lighthouse for the Pacific and Asia. For some time, we had grown increasingly aware of the great needs of this area, the least evan- gelized region in the entire world. Sixty percent of the earth lived here, yet only one percent of Asia claimed a personal relationship with Christ.

We *both* now knew the direction of our next adventure. We'd be expanding our horizon. Hawaii, after all, was a stepping stone to Asia.

"We'll move to the Big Island, permanently!" I said.

Dar laughed when I said the word "permanently," thinking of our nine years together, spent in tents, schoolrooms and camps. Why, our kids' home was almost literally a suitcase with pictures of their family attached to the inside lid. I laughed with her, suddenly relieved that we saw the path ahead again clearly.

It was just as well that neither of us knew just how hard it would be to claim that spot of ground for our stepping stone into Asia.

Chapter Sixteen

Kalafi Comes Home

Something was happening! I could feel it in the air. It was three years after Darlene and I and the children said goodbye to our home in Lausanne, three years after Dar had left her favorite wildflowers in the fields around the Lausanne hotel, substituting for them the brilliant flowers of Hawaii's Big Island.

I turned the YWAM van onto the access road leading to the tumbling-down buildings, half-hidden by a jungle of bushes and weeds. The sign on the main road, with some letters missing, read "Pacific Empress Hotel." Darlene and I, Karen and David, eight and six now, sat squeezed together in the front seat. Ten more YWAMers were crowded into the back of the van. Three other vehicles followed close behind. We were all dressed in our oldest clothes for the dirty job ahead. When we got to the pot-holed parking lot, Karen summed it up.

"What a mess!"

And yet I am sure we were all seeing this property with other eyes too. The Lord was at work. I looked at the tangle of tropical vines that half-obscured the quadrangle of buildings which eight years ago, before their bankruptcy, had been the Pacific Empress Hotel. The gently sloping 45 acres surrounding the property had once been the hotel's golf course. We had secured all this, in its prime location, with just a little money down.

"At least we have a beautiful view," offered Dar. She was certainly right! Above us was the peak of Hualalei, the extinct volcano, which gave us abundantly rich land. Below us was the panorama of glittering, turquoise, Kona Bay. I could just imagine a large white ship anchored there.

We went to work clearing the overgrowth. Hefting a machete and hoe, I plunged into what had once been a landscaped tropical garden around the swimming pool. All over the property volunteers from among the hundred staff and students at our present School of Evangelism were attacking the mess.

As I fell into the rhythm of hoeing, kneeling, and pulling the fist-thick weeds, I began to think about the quite remarkable results of that all-night seeking session, four years ago now, in the Kaneohe camp.

With one puzzling exception everything God had shown us in Kaneohe had come to pass. We were, indeed, on the Big Island. More pinpointedly, we were on the Kona coast of the Big Island just as the fellow with the blond beard had predicted. And, as foreseen that night, we now owned a 55-acre farm; a man had walked up to me and said God had told him to give it to us. And the large white house on the hill that we had seen? That was now YWAM property, too, housing staff and students for our new Discipleship Training Schools.

It seemed on the surface that we were fulfilling our mandate. Why then were Darlene and I still restless? It just didn't make sense, I said to myself as I pulled another fistful of weeds growing in the lava. Yet over the last three years here on the Big Island both of us had felt there was something more. One day—about a year before—I found out why when a question formed in my mind, "Loren, have you checked your life lately against your original call?"

It was a principle of guidance that I had been neglecting. Regularly we ought to check our progress against our original mandates. My calling was clear: to preach the twin character of the gospel. Through Jesus it is possible to love God with all our hearts and to love our neighbors as ourselves.

How successful—I'd asked myself during that review time— had we been in taking that twin love to all the world?

We'd not done too good a job, I felt, reaching our neighbor at the point where he was hurting. Ever since the Bahamas I'd dreamed of a ship that would go on mercy missions, helping us love our neighbor in his needs. Our first effort had been put on the altar because it robbed Jesus of His glory. But there'd been encouragements to hold onto our dream. One in particular meant a lot to me: somewhere in our packed boxes, waiting for a wall to hang on, was a plaque my mother had sent me. It said, "Don't Give Up the Ship."

And the identical twin, learning to love God with all our hearts and minds and strength? We had been hard at work in this area. The Good News had often been communicated by Christians in "religious" settings, usually large meetings in a church somewhere. But the secular world was using so many other ways to communicate its messages: the arts, entertainment, family, education, media, business, government.

Suddenly—that day a year ago as I was touching base with my original calling—the vision expanded.

Suppose—my heart had raced—suppose we trained young people, especially Asians and Pacific islanders, in these very same strategic areas of communication. Our purpose would be to release thousands of young people into these mind-molding streams of society as a multiplication factor for missions. In our training we'd stress relationships as much as head knowledge . . . relationships with God and with each other. We would use a floating faculty of experts who would come alternately to live with the students in the village lifestyle of Asia and the Pacific. The emphasis would be on learning through doing.

And now here we were, standing on the grounds of our "university."

"You do have a sense of humor, Lord," I said above the swish-chop noise of my machete as I hacked through a bougainvillaea bush. "Only You could be creative enough to take this old hotel and turn it into a university." I thought, though, of the way Harvard, Yale and Princeton had started as equally struggling dreams by men who wished to focus on the gospel. It seemed an ongoing process. Now PACU, the Pacific and Asia Christian University, would be in the grand tradition in one respect at least—we were starting with nothing but a conviction and a Lord who guides.

Yet, for now we were beginning the horrendous challenge of clearing land and repairing buildings of the old hotel. David ran up to me with six-year-old excitement about a tractor that had just arrived.

"Come look, Daddy! The tractor is pulling up the prickly bushes with a chain. Come look!"

Gratefully, I put down my machete and took David's hand and walked with him toward the welcome tractor. In that brief moment I saw into tomorrow. I saw the day when thousands of young men and women would walk over these same grounds and out into the world as missionaries, communicators of God's grace.

If the grounds were a problem, the buildings were worse. Dar and I and the children walked through the dilapidated quadrangle of the old hotel.

"Do you realize there are 99 rooms here and 100 toilets!" I said to Darlene.

"And all of them," Dar said with a shudder, "are a mess!"

Our family had a special goal for that afternoon. We needed to find some rooms in the complex to serve as our home. Frankly, nothing seemed attractive. Every one of the four buildings was in acute disrepair. Much of the wood was termite-ridden and some rooms reeked of urine from the squatters who occupied the hotel until we bought it. Rats and cockroaches came and went as they pleased.

"I told you you'd be living very simply if you married me, Dar. But *this?*" I said, sweeping my arm to indicate a pile of rotting debris. "I don't see how even you can make the children feel at home here." I spoke laughingly, tousling Karen's hair, but I really wondered how Dar would manage. We had been married 14 years and we didn't even have a car or furniture of our own. Since coming to the Hawaiian islands, Dar and I and the children had moved 18 times. Eighteen moves in three years!

"Don't worry, Loren," Dar said, "it'll look totally different when it's cleaned up!"

Dar finally chose three third-floor motel rooms. They had adjoining doors and a carpet that had once been blue. When we walked into the bathroom, I thought the fixtures had never been cleaned!

But how eager our YWAMers were to help. Over the next two weeks scores of young people pitched in. The girls cleaned the toilets—all 100 of them. The boys specialized in shampooing the filthy carpets. We had shifts of young men working all day and all night, going from room to room with a shampooer we'd rented from Pay'n Save.

But at last Darlene and I and the children moved up the hill from our last quarters downtown in the village of Kailua-Kona. We plopped our suitcases down on the now-brightly-cleaned blue carpet and looked out through the picture window, over the coconut palm trees, toward the gleaming bay. Dar was already getting out the children's cup, bowl and pictures. "Here we are kids," she said handing Karen and David their precious ongoing symbols. "Let's make ourselves a home."

A few days after moving in, I sat on a borrowed, folding canvas chair on our porch—or lanai, as we call it in Hawaii—talking with a professor named Dr. Howard Malmstadt.

One of the principles we use in seeking guidance is *ongoing confirmation,* similar to the road signs you would look for on an unfamiliar highway. It was while we were sitting there on those folding canvas chairs that I saw just such a sign. Howard Malmstadt was a leading scientist and professor at the University of Illinois at Urbana campus when I first met him.

Now, as we sat on the lanai, I told Howard that God had been leading us toward a university. It would be a very special kind of spawning place, helping young people know God and then make Him known in the influential areas of society.

"I know," he said quietly. "God already told me."

Howard went on to explain that he had recently been asked to allow his name to be considered for the presidency of a Midwestern university. When he prayed about the offer, though, a startling thought dropped into his mind: He was to go to Hawaii instead. "Why Hawaii?" "Because," God answered, "I am going to give a university to YWAM. It will be in Hawaii and you will be a part of it."

As encouraging as these clear directions were, other areas

gave far less comfort. The most wrenching of these was in the life of our dear Kalafi. For two years Kalafi had fallen into the worst troubles imaginable.

I'd heard the first warning bell about Kalafi four years earlier, in 1973, at the Osaka conference when he spoke of problems in his marriage with Tapu. Dar and I met with them at our next conference, a year later. We found a quiet room, closed the door and heard their sad story. The "marital problem," we learned, had been a girl.

"I kissed her, Loren. It never went any further than that! I confessed it to Tapu and to the other leaders under me. I thought it was over."

But Tapu had been deeply wounded. She couldn't forget the betrayal. There was more, details Dar and I didn't want to hear. We prayed with both of them; they cried and spoke words of contrition. At first we thought it was over and done with, but something wasn't right. I couldn't define it myself, but I knew there was still a weakness. I tried to get Kalafi and Tapu to stay on with us in Hawaii, to be part of the next school but Kalafi refused. "No," he said, "we've been offered a free house in California. I think we should drop out of ministry for a while. We want to get our marriage together again. . . ." It didn't sound altogether right to me somehow but I didn't insist.

Within weeks of their arriving in California, our worst fears came true. Word came from the parents of a girl Kalafi had started seeing on the Mainland. They were afraid their daughter and Kalafi were having an affair. Tapu, I learned, was also seeing someone else. I flew to Los Angeles to talk to Kalafi. Although I gave him every chance to speak honestly, he chose not to do so. From his lighthearted banter, I almost believed I had heard unfounded rumors.

When I got to the Big Island, however, I received another call from the parents of the girl. I knew now that I had to confront my friend. I reached him at home. "Kalafi," I said, my voice echoing over the trans-Pacific line, "you must realize the seriousness of what you're doing! Come back now. It's still not too late."

His response was an awful silence.

The next week, I got a letter. I tore it open and read, "I respect God, Loren, but I can't be a hypocrite. I need to live my own life. Please don't try to contact me again for a while."

Tears stung my eyes. But I wasn't giving up. I remembered another time when persistence had mended a broken relationship—when I kept calling my Aunt Arnette in Miami until at last she agreed to see me.

A few months after Kalafi's letter, I saw Joy Dawson again and we picked up our intercessory prayer for Kalafi. "God give him another chance! " we begged, unashamed of the tears running down our cheeks. At this very time, we found out later, Kalafi was in a bar with several other young men. He had quickly plunged into sin, becoming the first each night to start drinking and the last to remain standing in the fights that often broke out. He had even started carrying a gun. On this night, he was in his favorite bar doing his best to get fighting-drunk when a slip of a girl scooted into the booth beside him. Above the raucous music the girl began to tell Kalafi how she had once gone forward in a Billy Graham meeting. Kalafi looked at her in surprise: none of his new friends knew his background. The girl told Kalafi she wished she had stuck with that decision.

"Kalafi, I'm so afraid," she finished. "I know I'm going to die and go to hell! "

At this Kalafi roared, shouting above the din of the barroom the astonishing words, *"God, get off my back!"*

Darlene and I were again in Los Angeles. We decided to go to Kalafi's house on the off chance that we'd find him at home. Our timing was amazing. We arrived just as Kalafi came to collect his belongings; he was moving out for good. I saw a hardness I had never known existed. And Tapu, we asked? Kalafi kept on packing. All he knew was that Tapu was singing in a nightclub in Inglewood. He didn't know where she was living, but he thought it might be an apartment on one of the north-south boulevards.

Dar and I drove to Inglewood feeling stupid. How could we ever find anyone in this maze of apartments? "God, you know where Tapu is," I prayed. "Would you please lead us to her?"

How can I describe what happened next? It took me a long time even to believe it myself. We were driving east along Imperial Boulevard, praying that God would show us which street to turn on. I crossed Inglewood Avenue and came to Hawthorne Boulevard, and felt I should turn back to Inglewood Avenue. "Yes," said Dar, "that's right." I turned south onto Inglewood Avenue, driving four blocks, slowly. Then the Holy Spirit's voice spoke into my mind. *Stop here.*

"Let's try that one," I said. Dar agreed right away. The apartment was a fading, green stucco two-story building—almost identical with a dozen on both sides of the boulevard.

We got out, stepping over broken toys and bicycles on the sidewalk. We found a little girl who said yes, a woman matching our description lived in an apartment on the second floor. We walked up the stairs and knocked.

Tapu opened the door, clutching her bathrobe. Her eyes widened and she backed into her living room. "How ever did you find me! Come in but I can't talk. I have to go!"

We pleaded with Tapu but it was useless. After a five minute visit, standing awkwardly in her living room, we left.

The very next week Joy Dawson felt she should write Kalafi one more letter. It arrived, we learned later, the day before Kalafi planned a party complete with drugs. Kalafi picked up Joy's letter at the post office, took it to his car and tore it open. Suddenly God spoke to him. Kalafi could hear Him with his natural ears, and he began sweating all over. "Kalafi," the Lord said tenderly, "living the Christian life is difficult. There is only one thing harder— that's not being a Christian. The price that you pay to follow Me is far less than the price you'll have to pay not to follow Me."

Kalafi found the nearest phone booth and called me on the Big Island. He contacted the Dawsons, praying with them for hours, ending five months of separation from God. Then he came back to Hawaii. I sensed he needed time to heal. At my encouragement, he enrolled in the University of Hawaii on the other side of the Big Island. In his spare time Kalafi started a landscape business which was soon flourishing. Kalafi never did things by halves!

He told me on a visit to our side of the Big Island that he

never expected to have a ministry again. "It'll be enough if Jesus forgives me," he said. "I just need to *be* for a while, not *do.*"

Watching Kalafi's progress over the next year and a half meant at times watching him fall backwards. Kalafi and Tapu tried to get back together . . . the effort failed. They called it quits and were divorced. Kalafi began drinking a bit again. When I confronted him he asked me to leave him alone. Shortly, we learned that he had re-married. Leda, his new wife, was not a Christian.

All the while we were having to walk such a tightrope, choosing where to confront, where to give a loose rein. Kalafi had come into YWAM before our training schools got started, so he had not experienced that discipline before being thrust into leadership. In a way what we were going through now was an individualized crash course.

"The only thing is," I said to Dar one night when we were stretched out on the floor in our living room interceding for Kalafi, "I sometimes wonder if he will pass the course."

One special, special day, nine months after we had heard that Kalafi had re-married, I received a telephone call.

"Could Leda and I come over for a visit with you?" Kalafi asked.

Could they come over? Need he ask? Nothing would thrill our hearts more. "Yes, yes," I said. "Friday night?"

So Kalafi and Leda, who was pregnant, arrived for dinner. Joy Dawson had been teaching at our school on the Big Island and this was her last evening with us. After our meal, Joy took Kalafi aside while Dar talked to Leda. Like a flower exposed to sunlight, Leda immediately opened up to receive Jesus. We were so excited.

I looked across the room where Joy was in earnest conversation with Kalafi. I could see by his hunched shoulders and furrowed brow that he was weighing his total surrender to God. As he left that night, I knew Kalafi's destiny was still hanging in the balance. He knew too much of God and had experienced too much of Him ever to live in mediocrity.

A few weeks later Kalafi called again. This time, he asked if he could see me privately.

I saw to my relief, as Kalafi sat with head bowed and hands folded, that he was ready to make a clear-cut choice to obey God. He poured out hurts and guilts he had been harboring for years. It was a sad, familiar tale of lust and pride, which he had never been able to confess fully. We both wept. As I stood beside Kalafi to pray with him, I knew that here, in spite of the struggles, was a young man God wanted to use.

Kalafi decided that he had to write letters to all of the churches and YWAM bases where he had ministered over the years, telling them frankly of his sins and asking for forgiveness. He also wrote to Tapu asking her forgiveness, and to his own family back in Tonga.

Then one of the more intriguing forms of guidance began to take place.

Kalafi's landscaping business suddenly went sour.

Kalafi had taken on two major jobs, but now, unexplainably, he met delay after delay. A bulldozer would break down; he would hire another; in an hour or two it too would break down. After five such mishaps Kalafi began to wonder! Then a friend called inviting Kalafi to speak at a Saturday night Bible study class in a nearby church. At first he did not want to go, but Leda encouraged him.

"They're not asking you to preach, Kalafi. They just want you to tell what's been happening."

So Kalafi did go. That Saturday night he stood in the sanctuary of this church, telling how he had tried to walk away from the Lord, how he had committed adultery, how his marriage had broken up, and how God was now leading him back.

As he spoke Kalafi began to weep. To his amazement, a man in the first row fell to his knees beside his chair. Then another did the same. People all over the church were weeping. Several gave their lives to Jesus that night, others had broken marriages restored.

After that powerful night, Kalafi knew God was giving him back his ministry. He and Leda soon began to visit us regularly on Friday nights. They were always brimming with news. Kalafi finally got the message from the broken-down bulldozers and gave up his business; he and Leda were now living on whatever God provided. They began conducting a Christian fellowship every Friday night, leading people to Christ and seeing broken bodies and minds mended.

I wondered about Kalafi's ministry after his divorce and remarriage. It seemed clear to me that although divorce is not in God's perfect plan it is not the unpardonable sin either since God had restored Kalafi's ministry. If being perfectly at the heart of His will were the criterion for ministry, how many of us would qualify? Fortunately, even when we fail God does not take back His gifts and callings.

It was exciting watching Kalafi come back to fruitfulness and at the same time we were watching the campus of our future university slowly emerge from beneath the tropical overgrowth.

To be honest, with all of this going on, I'd just about forgotten the one remaining element in that all-night seeking session we held in Kaneohe nearly four years ago. Those prophecies also included seeing a ship in harbor on Kona.

That, however, was a suppression of memory which wasn't going to last long.

Chapter Seventeen

Don't Give Up The Ship

One day, about two months after Dar and I moved into our rooms at the hotel in Kona, I was on a trip visiting with Don Stephens.

"Loren," Don said, "I wonder if God might not be stirring up the ship vision again."

My reaction was immediate. "Oh, no!" I mumbled, just under my breath, "not another ship!" That would be two major projects at the same time—the university and the ship.

Don didn't hear my mumbling. He went on to describe a ship he had located in Venice, Italy. "It's called the *Victoria*," Don said, his eyes alive. "I've taken several European team members to see it, though I sometimes wonder why. It is a huge old thing and it has no lights . . . the generator isn't even running. It's just a big eleven thousand ton passenger liner, dead in the water.

"But Loren," Don ran on excitedly, "the ship could be bought for a song precisely because it is in such bad shape. There'd be lots of repairs but we could handle that, don't you think?"

I'm afraid I said nothing at all.

"Well," Don finished lamely, dampened by my lack of response, "there *was* something special about the *Victoria*. . . . "

Looking for something to say I asked, "What color is the ship, Don?"

"White," he replied.

For the first time since this conversation began my heart skipped a beat. The ship we'd "seen" in the bay in our all-night prayer meeting in Kaneohe . . . that ship was white, too.

About two months later a man came to the Big Island and asked around until he found out where we lived. He was in my office at the hotel now, looking out over the now freshly land-scaped tropical foliage.

"Paul Ainsworth's my name. From Toronto."

He began to shift uneasily on the folding canvas chair. I smiled, trying to put him at ease. "Frankly, sir," Mr. Ainsworth went on, "I don't really know why I'm here except that I've had a very strange experience and somehow it may involve you. You see, sir, I've . . . well . . . I've had a vision."

I was becoming interested. Mr. Ainsworth stumbled on. He told me how a few days earlier he had been at a prayer meeting in Toronto. All of a sudden in front of his eyes he saw a map of the South Pacific. There was a large white ship coming across his vision. The ship seemed to be sailing from the Hawaiian Islands, heading south.

I was suddenly *very* interested.

"I could read the names of the islands on the map," Mr. Ainsworth said. "Someone in the prayer meeting got out an atlas and started following the route I was describing in my vision. Everything matched."

I was now sitting on the very edge of my own canvas chair. Mr. Ainsworth's next words sent chills through me. "As the ship moved through the Pacific," he said, "a revival broke out. Thousands of South Sea islanders came to Jesus and then they themselves became evangelists. They went into Southeast Asia, right up into India, and on into China. Millions came to know the Lord."

The vision had lasted for two hours, Paul Ainsworth said, and some of the details he told me didn't seem to apply to us.

"What do you want me to do now, Lord?" he had asked God. The Lord said, "Go to Hawaii." Mr. Ainsworth knew no one in Hawaii, but in obedience he made travel plans. Before he left a friend handed him a piece of paper saying, "This man may help you. He lives in Hawaii." Paul Ainsworth opened the note on the plane. All it said was *Loren Cunningham*.

I could hardly believe what I was hearing. Mr. Ainsworth was now studying my face, waiting no doubt for some indication that this all made sense. I was near tears myself but I walked over and picked up the plaque my mother had given me. I showed it to him and then had the unusual pleasure of telling this obedient man our entire story. We both started to laugh the way I have seen Polynesians laugh, out of sheer nervousness. Mother's plaque, of course, said, "Don't Give Up the Ship."

Everything was happening too quickly and too spectacularly and the amazing series was not over yet. After Mr. Ainsworth's visit Darlene received a letter from an old friend, who spent much time in intercession for YWAM, who wrote, "The Lord told me you and Loren are giving birth to twins. Not literally, I'm sure. I believe the twins are *ministries*. One is the ship. I'm not sure what the other one is. . . ."

Everywhere we were hearing about twins! Some could hardly be called divine guidance, but were fun to think about anyhow. My mind ran back to the delightful day, a few months earlier, when Jimmy and Jannie finally had a family after 11 years of marriage. On the day of the birth we were all surprised when Jannie gave birth to identical twin boys, born seven minutes apart on 7-7-'77. It did seem that God was saying something to us about twins.

After such a stunning series of Bible-story-like encouragements, we just had to plunge ahead with negotiations for the purchase of the *Victoria*. I suppose God had to be so overwhelmingly obvious with me because He knew I might give up otherwise. How was He ever going to release enough money to accomplish such a mission?

Three months after Don first spoke to me about it, we decided to begin negotiations with the owners of the *Victoria*. I couldn't help but laugh at the contrast between talking deposits and pay outs and escrows on the one hand and on the other watching Dar wash our dishes in the bathroom sink at our motel room.

Don sent me a picture of the ship along with a diagram of the vessel. But I have to admit that after the experience with the *Maori*, I put the diagram in a drawer.

Then a month later, in April 1978, I flew to Venice to meet with Don Stephens. It was a two-purpose visit. Four hundred YWAMers were here talking to people about Jesus on the streets of Venice; they were living in a campground on the outskirts of the city. But of course I was especially interested in Venice because that was where the *Victoria* was berthed.

As Don drove me from the airport, he updated me on the negotiations. The owners were considering our offer, submitted a month earlier, and had even sought government approval for the sale if they should decide to go ahead.

"These people did not take us seriously at first," said Don as we snaked through traffic, "and I can't blame them. We're so naive about shipping we had to ask them which questions to ask. We were embarrassed to give our address, care of a campground!"

We drove down the causeway linking Venice to the mainland and then pulled off the road. Don pointed toward the dockside cranes.

"There she is."

In spite of myself I must admit my heart raced. There she lay with her orange and black smokestack. "And the symbol on the stack," Don was saying, "is the Lion of St. Mark the Evangelist, patron saint of Venice. Interesting, no?"

I'm not sure that Don understood my reluctance, but I just did not want to go aboard the ship right then. The trouble was that I might become *too* excited. After the experience with the *Maori*, the last thing I wanted to do was exalt another piece of metal.

But I was certainly open to letting the Lord work through Don and the other men. For me personally, it was a matter of keeping a balance between the spiritual caution I'd learned from the *Maori* and the boldness I'd gained from hearing Paul Ainsworth's vision.

So I encouraged Don to go ahead. When he related the overwhelming task to be done I could only say, "Don, let's break the job down into small units so we can handle it. God never expects us to take more than one step at a time."

I went home with a mixture of excitement and concern. Darlene and I kept coming back to the same question, "Is that really You, Lord?" We had seen before, at times of great turning points, that it helps to ask ourselves, "How much of the supernatural is there in the guidance we are receiving?" We had not been asking for signs, nor seeking the spectacular, but signs and spectacular coincidences had been occurring one after another and it seemed spiritual foolishness not to pay attention! God was probably saying, "This is the way, walk in it."

So Don went ahead with the negotiations. A month later he telephoned from Venice, all excited. The ship owners had approved our offer: government authorities were in accord.

"You should have seen us, Loren!" Don reported. "Everybody wanted to go down for the signing. Five of us crowded into a tiny French Renault 4 and drove out of a campground to sign for a ship!"

So we had our contract. We scraped up money for the down payment from funds raised within YWAM. But something other than money was being released here, something that was at the very heart of our original concept of Youth With A Mission.

One of the most trustworthy tests for valid guidance is this: does it bring the people who are involved one step closer to freedom and maturity in the Lord? If this is not so, the guidance is probably suspect. If it is so, the direction is probably from God. In this particular instance, Don Stephens was the principal person being released. He had proven himself in Munich and now he was being given a far tougher mission.

All the while, like binoculars coming into focus, our university concept was becoming clearer. Dr. Howard Malmstadt, the professor who came to our doorstep, had indeed stayed on just as God had indicated. He and I now spent hours lying on the blue carpet of our apartment, praying and planning and brainstorming. Howard introduced me to an architect who peppered us with questions about the relationship-oriented lifestyle plans for PACU. We explained to him that students, staff, visiting teachers and their families would all live together in villages, with 280 people each. We wanted to do this because most of the students were to be Asian and Pacific islanders, and at home they lived in villages. We told the architect about the colleges which were forming around the "mind-molders," those areas which shape a society and culture. The campus needed to be designed to encourage a live-learn environment within these colleges. Our architect was excited by the challenge. He flew back to the mainland and began to draw up the campus design, donating it as a labor of love.

I worried a lot about the size of the two commitments we were facing. I worried about the money, of course, but that wasn't my real concern. . . .

Our efforts at being led by the Lord had revealed a danger area in guidance. Divine guidance is so heady, so spectacular, that there is the risk of glory attaching itself to the work rather than to the Lord. We made that mistake with the *Maori* and we were not going to let it happen again!

But a second danger area showed up now. When God guides us He is taking a risk, too. If we make the wrong choices we can end up not only robbing Him of His *glory* but of His rightful *first attention*.

Without realizing it I was about to head into this second danger zone. Ever since Munich we'd made an effort to be at major international sporting events. They were miniature worlds, often even giving us opportunities to meet people from "closed" countries. One such event was the World Cup Soccer Games to be held over a four-week period in Argentina in June 1978 only eight weeks away. I made preparations to go, satisfied that God wanted me there.

Then, shortly before my departure for the World Cup, a friend phoned from the Mainland.

"Loren, I've got the best news. I've met a real estate developer who wants to give a lot of money for a Christian university," he said excitedly. "He'd like to meet with you. He's in Denver."

This could get the university going sooner than we thought! I'd be a day or two late getting to the World Cup, maybe, but on the other hand. . . .

"I'll swing by and visit him on my way to Argentina," I said, trying to keep my voice calm.

So, on the day I was supposed to fly to Buenos Aires, I few instead to Denver. After delays, I finally arrived in Argentina. The Games were two-thirds through. I met with the teams and tried to make up for lost time with extra enthusiasm. But the respectful, polite mood of the young people was like that of a youngster playing in the finals of a high school football season only to have Dad show up in the third quarter because he'd been at an important meeting. The mood of our staff, too, was worrisome. When I explained where I'd been, no one was impressed. *This* was the event we'd all been led to, and though no one said so outright, I knew that I had some thinking to do.

That night—very late—in my room in the school in Buenos Aires where 700 of us were being housed, I began to think about the guidance factors involved in this experience.

There was no doubt in my mind that the university was a dream dear to the heart of God. It was a fresh way of sending waves of young people into new mission fields, the mind-molding centers of our society. But the *Maori* had been a tool close to the heart of God, too. I still believed that. Yet He let the ship die because it was becoming a glorious thing all in itself.

With the university, God's call for our attention was threatened in an even more serious way. He had told me to be in Argentina. I heard the directions clearly. But I ended up chasing after money instead.

This is when I first wished I had a wall-hanging that said *Guidance is first of all a relationship with the Guide.*

The first goal of guidance is to lead us into a closer relationship with Jesus. All other goals should be subservient to that.

We have to be especially watchful when He is leading us toward *tools,* such as a ship or a university. There is nothing wrong with tools. But it's a sad day if the tools ever supersede the Lord Himself.

Chapter Eighteen

"Doesn't Anybody Care?"

Don Stephens called Dar and me late one evening seven months after we began negotiating for the *Victoria*. Dar had managed in the year we'd been in our apartment at the Kona hotel, to make the three rooms into a home. She was beginning to accumulate a chair here, a lamp there.

"Well, Loren, it's done," Don's voice came in over the satellite telephone. He seemed excited and yet strangely subdued.

"We have a ship?" I asked. Dar perked up from across the room. For months now money had been coming in with encouraging regularity. It was, we felt, a major part of our guidance.

"We have a ship. She's not seaworthy, but she's ours. The owners waited until the last dollar was in before they let the ship go."

Don said they'd be holding a candlelight thanksgiving feast in the ship's dining room then they'd go to the afterdeck to lower the ensign and replace it with our own.

"Of course our problems have just begun, Loren," Don said. No wonder he seemed both excited and subdued. "Sooner or later we'll have to leave Venice because we have a non-union crew. We'll have to be towed somewhere for dry docking. Probably Greece."

"Don," I said, feeling that I needed to shift the conversation, "what do you think of the new name by now?"

"The *Anastasis*?" That was the name we'd liked. "Yes, it seems right."

"The *Anastasis* it is then," I said, looking at Dar who was listening to one side of the phone conversation, glad that she was smiling her agreement.

Anastasis is the Greek word for resurrection.

One of the problems with being led by the Lord is keeping perspective. As divine guidance begins to unfold, it always seems to come with hard, gritty work. Gone is the thrill of the original leading. Ahead, still, is the excitement of seeing the fruit of this same leading. All that's left in between is mind-numbing, muscle-straining labor. It is in this interim period that the Perspective Principle becomes so important.

It was June 1979; a year had passed since I first saw "our" ship and as my Alitalia flight circled the canals of Venice I craned my neck to catch a glimpse of her. Some sixty of us were gathering in Venice. Don needed to see as many of the YWAM leaders from around the world as possible, so that we could reassure him of our support. And we needed to re-kindle our vision of a ship going out in Jesus' name.

My eyes scanned the sparkling waters. There she lay in the glare of the Venetian sun—still with her rather shabby coat of white paint, but now with a blue and green smokestack. Half an hour later a sleek water taxi was bouncing over the harbor toward our ship. I could pick out the freshly-painted YWAM logo on the smokestack. We rounded the stern to come alongside the gang-plank. The old name had been painted over and now, emblazoned across the stern in black letters was the word, *Anastasis*.

As I stepped on deck, Don and his volunteer workers—most of whom were quite young—greeted me warmly. I had been reluctant to come aboard until we knew there was no turning back, still determined not to glorify a mere tool in God's Kingdom. But now I was glad to be here, taking the tour of the 522-foot vessel, its large dining rooms, forward lounge, small hospital unit and five large cargo holds. I could see where young volunteers had been scraping, sanding, repairing, painting. The galley alone, Don said, took 25 young people three weeks to clean.

By now other leaders were coming on board. Sixty of us gathered on the promenade deck where passengers formerly sunbathed during long ocean voyages. Don began to tell us of the complexities of towing the ship to Athens and preparing her for operation. We prayed over these problems, putting the Perspective Principle to work by recalling both the original vision and the future potential of a ship as an evangelistic and Mercy Ministry tool. We would need this to carry us through the long hard months ahead.

The visit to the *Anastasis* was over. As our launch pulled away I think all of us felt a renewed understanding of God's yearning for His people to be involved in Mercy Ministry. What pleased me was that the next step thrusting YWAM into these needs came from a brand new generation, the 27-year-old son of Jim and Joy Dawson.

"Loren," John Dawson said to me, back in the States, "God has been speaking to me . . . and I think His message is for all of us in YWAM."

He had my attention instantly. This young man had lots of family experience hearing the voice of God. John went on to relate how he had recently read an article in *Time* magazine about refugees fleeing Vietnam.

"Loren," John said, "these Boat People pay outrageous sums for leaky tubs to try to get out of Vietnam. Then they are pirated and shot or left adrift on rafts." Nobody wanted to help these people. He described the over-crowded refugee camps in neighboring countries. "Loren, I couldn't get away from the title of the article, This is the world's question to the Body of Christ. That's how God must feel about these people. He's sobbing, 'Doesn't Anyone Care?'"

John's challenge began to haunt me. Was this at last the beginning of the Mercy Missions I had envisioned ever since Hurricane Cleo fifteen years ago?

I decided to have a look for myself. Taking a few other YWAM leaders, we went to Hong Kong and then to Thailand. The first refugee camp we visited was in Hong Kong. No magazine articles could prepare eyes and ears—or nose—for the shock of that scene in Camp Jubilee.

The smell came first. The brown stench of raw human waste hit us before we entered the place. As we walked in the main entrance, into an inner passageway, we found the source. The lower floor of the building was eight inches deep in human waste. We picked our way around the perimeter as best we could, camp officials pointing to some broken sewer pipes along the side of the wall. There was not enough money to hire a plumber from the city and no one there who was qualified or willing to tackle the huge mess.

Jubilee Camp was a former police barracks designed to hold 900. Now the condemned structure held 8,000. There was simply no other place to put the overwhelming number of refugees. Each room held wall-to-wall bunks, three high, with several families living in each tier. One family would occupy two bunks: not just for sleeping, but for everything including cooking. The doctors of the camp, pitifully overworked, told how everyday they would treat the concussions of small children who had fallen from high bunks in their sleep.

Already my mind was busy. Did we have to wait? We could bring workers here even before the *Anastasis* was under sail. We could help clean up the mess, help care for the sick, and also have a chance to share the message of Jesus with these people—that He cared about their suffering and wanted to do something about it. We would be sharing His love with one hand and His truth with the other.

The concern and strange excitement that we felt in Hong Kong we also felt in Thailand. I watched a Hmong mother hold out the skeletal frame of a baby boy with his too-large head lolling backwards. Food had come too late for him. My stomach knotted as I heard the rattle in his tiny throat; my eyes filled as he drew his last shuddering breath and his mother clasped his lifeless body to her. *Where?* I screamed inside of myself, *Where is the Church of Jesus Christ?*

A moment later I looked into the eyes of a youthful Khmer Rouge soldier. He might have been one of those who had thrown a baby into the air and caught him on the point of his bayonet. The young man's eyes were vacant, gaping portholes into hell itself. But Jesus had died for this man, too. Through an interpreter, I spoke with 1,200 of the Khmer Rouge in that camp. Many listened intently to our account of God's love, forgiveness and call to repentance. Two dozen men came apart with me to pray, at no little risk to their own safety.

When I returned to Kona I felt a deep heaviness but I also felt great excitement and a sense of completion. At last we were coming full circle with our Ministry of Mercy at YWAM. The long-awaited twins of the good news—an ever-deeper love of God and an ever-deeper love for our neighbor—were at last really being brought into the world.

Within weeks we had young people out in the refugee camps. Gary Stephens (Don's younger brother) led a group of thirty into Jubilee Camp. They did what even the refugees had been unwilling to do: shoveled out all the human waste, repaired the broken sewage pipes, fixed the toilets. Gary reported back that the refugees marveled. Here were young people who were paying their own way to come and do a job no one else would consider. The YWAMers had their attention, all right! Time after time they were given the lead they hoped for: they were asked why they had come.

Soon the team had permission from camp officials to open a school, hold Bible study classes, offer counseling.

Then an amazing thing happened. It seemed like God had been waiting for this particular obedience to open His store-house. As word spread of our finally-released emphasis on the second twin, workers streamed to us. It was as if we had opened a door against which hundreds of young men and women had been pressed, waiting. More experienced people came too. Doctors, nurses and technical experts as well as people willing to roll bandages or teach refugee youths. Soon we found a dozen opportunities—vocational rehabilitation, cottage industries, food and clothing distribution, English classes and cultural re-orientation for those headed for a new life. And all the while both with our actions and our words we were spreading the gospel message, leading people to their Heavenly Father.

The blessings of God flowed elsewhere as well. Kalafi was doing well in his newly-regained ministry. The old fire was back, along with a new tenderness, gained after his own fall. He had started schools in Honolulu, Singapore and Djakarta, training young evangelists. Stories drifted back of hundreds being saved;

and of healings—a deaf girl instantly hearing in Malaysia, an old crippled Moslem in Indonesia running and jumping after Kalafi prayed for him; and of churches being formed in unreached villages. We positively glowed over these reports which showed Kalafi's complete restoration.

It seemed that God was heaping blessings on top of blessings now. Like Jim and Jannie's story, I smiled to myself. They had waited 11 years, then their twins were born. Now they also had a third boy—an added, special gift.

And that's the way it was in YWAM as well, all over the world God was adding more and more gifts, multiplying releases.

One leader, Al Akimoff, sent two thousand into the Soviet Union in 1980 to proclaim the Gospel. Another man, Floyd McClung and his family moved in among the prostitutes, male and female, of the Red Light district of Amsterdam. Other men were becoming responsible for zones of the world: Africa, North and South America. The multiplication principle was at work, too: YWAMers in Brazil reported that young people trained in our Schools of Evangelism were now themselves pushing into their own frontiers, going up the Amazon to reach isolated Indian tribes with the gospel.

And our work, Darlene's and mine? As we had foreseen when we moved to Hawaii, our attention was turning toward Asia. We visited teams, joining in the evangelism, giving training to our growing family of 1,800 full-time workers. I still carried the weight of my own home base at Kona, believing firmly that the university was in God's heart. But instead of waiting for a campus and buildings we started *where we were*. The buildings were only tools, after all.

So the Pacific and Asia Christian University began. We rented a room here, a meeting hall there, an apartment somewhere else and began teaching.

In the meanwhile our other twin was still very much alive. As I would be discovering shortly.

Chapter Nineteen

A Fish Story

Halfway around the world, my friend Don Stephens and his team of 175 crew and students were trying to get the *Anastasis* ready to sail under her own steam. Don called me from Athens in early 1981. I was sitting on the lanai of our home at the school, looking out through the coconut palms toward the blueness of the bay. I could picture Don in Athens, calling from some anonymous phone booth. He briefed me on how his people were holding up.

"They are the heroes," Don said, bragging, as he always did, about his team. His young men and women had to worm their way into the stinking bilge of the ship to clean it. They scrubbed, scoured, polished, painted. And all of this with so little money that they could only buy generator oil for a few hours of electricity at a time. Their food was mostly peanut butter and rice and beans. The Athens port authorities would not let them live on board so they stayed in an old hotel that had been damaged in a recent earthquake. But just as in Hawaii we had decided not to wait on a *tool*, (the buildings and campus) before obeying God's call to start PACU, so also Don and his team in Athens decided not to wait for their tool (the ship) before obeying God's call to a Mercy Ministry. At every opportunity his teams were out helping Greek people suffering from the earthquake. They were also hard at work every day taking the gospel onto the streets right where they were.

I was pleased. "Don," I said, "we're getting the message aren't we? God wants us to focus our attention on His call, not on His tools."

All of YWAM began to help in the huge finances of the ship

itself but the kids under Don and Deyon continued to be responsible for their own support, usually through regular, non-begging, informative letters to folks back home. Very often the provision had an air of mystery about it. The kids would write to one person and get back a letter of encouragement from someone else— often someone they'd never heard of. Very often, funds too would come in from a totally unexpected direction.

The closer the *Anastasis* came to being seaworthy, the more often Don insisted on pulling back to basics. Why were the young people crawling between plates of the ship to clean it out? Because they were evangelists. They were already asking God for a huge harvest, thousands upon thousands of people who would be brought into His Kingdom, thousands more who would be helped in acts of mercy. In preparation for this releasing, Don became intrigued by the link between prayer-and-fasting and guidance to a good harvest. Jesus, after all, began His incredibly fruitful ministry after the wilderness fast. Perhaps the ship team should do the same!

So Don and Deyon and their 175 team members began a 40-day fast, rotating commitment so that at all times several people were doing the spiritual work of fasting and praying. I was fascinated, remembering the same kind of fasting-prayer in the Dawsons' New Zealand home immediately before the substantial release of workers from YWAM.

The 40-day spiritual discipline in Athens was just about over. One day the telephone rang. It was Don.

"Loren, are you ready?"

"Ready!" I could tell from the lightness in Don's voice that the news was good.

"Just make notes, good friend," Don said. "As soon as we began to see what was happening we took very accurate account and these figures are not exaggerated by even one fish. Listen to this. . . . " And then Don told the story of what happened as the crew was fasting and praying to be guided toward an abundant harvest.

One of the ship's crew was walking along the beach near the

hotel where the team lived. Suddenly he saw 12 medium-sized fish jump over the rocks into a shallow tidal pool right at his feet. He caught them and ran to the hotel to show the others. It was a big enough catch that a few staffers were able to have a fish fry to supplement their rice that night. A few days later, a large tuna jumped out of the sea onto the beach. This time more YWAMers got to eat a portion with their evening meal.

Again, a few days later, one of our young team members from Dallas, Texas, was having her quiet time seated on the rocks by the sea. Suddenly fish began to jump. She whooped and shouted. Local Greek families saw what was happening and ran up to catch the fish, too. Becky gathered 210 fish and the Greek families took two or three times that much home.

But the biggest fish story was yet to come.

"Just last Tuesday, Loren, at eight in the morning, the fish began jumping again!" Don and Deyon and the others ran, shouting down to the sea. For 150 yards downshore they could see fish leaping onto land. They ran back to the hotel and grabbed every container they could find—plastic buckets, dishpans, large bags. "Our crew spent 45 minutes gathering fish as fast as we could," Don said. What was causing them to leap up on the shore that way? Nobody knew. Their Greek friends had never seen anything like it. They said, "God is with these people."

When the great fishing party was over, they counted what they had been given in this unusual way. "Loren, you won't believe how many!" Don said. "There were 8,301—over one ton of fish, Loren! You can imagine the praise session we had right there on the beach. This was the encouragement we needed that the ministry of the *Anastasis* is going to be very, very special indeed."

Just as suddenly as the fish began to jump, signaling an abundant harvest for the *Anastasis'* Mercy Ministry, so was the final money released to pay for the technical work being done by the shipyard. Funds came in from all over the world. Hundreds of thousands of additional dollars were given sacrificially by YWAMers themselves and by groups such as 100 Huntley Street,

700 Club, PTL Club, the Billy Graham Evangelistic Association, David Wilkerson Youth Crusades, and Last Days Ministries.

There was no doubt about it. The ship ministry was in the process of being born.

And what about the university? We had at last found long-term financing but even so, a casual observer, strolling around the old grounds of the Pacific Empress Hotel, would hardly call this a university. We continued to press ahead anyhow. We dared not wait, in part because of a word given us by an obstetrician friend. He warned during one of our times of prayer for guidance that in the birth of twins the pregnancy had to be treated as *one*. When one twin is born the other must follow very rapidly or the life of the mother and the second twin will be jeopardized. He repeated again and again: we *must* see the second twin, PACU, born shortly or both the mother—YWAM—and the second twin would die.

This word encouraged us to continue our plans with or without buildings and a campus. Again, our early history was in the grand tradition. Oxford University, for instance, for years was an unglamorous collection of teachers and students getting together in whatever facilities they could find. In Kona, we had a few disciplines starting up already, including counseling, psychological training (from a biblical base), paramedical training, preschool teacher training, science, technology geared to the Third World, as well as schools of biblical study, missiology and church ministry. These colleges-in-embryo were sprinkled along the Kona Coast in whatever locations we could find.

The two ministries now were tracking each other closely. News of the firstborn was good. The *Anastasis'* sea trials in Athens had gone off without a hitch. Final procedures were underway for registering the vessel under the flag of Malta. This allowed us to sail with a non-union, international crew. Since we planned to have the crew of the *Anastasis* follow the usual YWAM pattern of depending on God for our own provision we could hardly comply with regulations of countries such as Italy where only unionized crews were recognized.

The great day finally came.

The *Anastasis* pulled up anchor and sailed from Greece on July 7, 1982. Was it an accident that this was the fifth birthday of Jim and Jannie's twins?

The ship was on its way to California.

Darlene and I, Karen and David, now aged fourteen and eleven, were in L.A. for the welcoming ceremony for the *Anastasis*. What a special occasion. The ship was steaming into the very city where YWAM had gotten its start.

I thought of how much had happened in the 22 years since we began with a dream in a bedroom-office. It had been a bumpy beginning. But so much had come full circle. I smiled as I recalled a recent meeting with Thomas Zimmerman, my former leader in the Assemblies of God. I told him now how much I loved and appreciated him, thanking him for the role he had played at a crucial time in my life. Perhaps without even realizing it he had helped me solidify the vision God had given me, that He wanted the waves of young people to go out from *every* denomination, not just my own. Before we parted, we both agreed it would be a good thing for him to come speak at our school in Kona in the near future. I shook his hand and said, "Thank you, Brother Zimmerman. . . ." He was indeed a dear brother.

Now I was standing among the 2,000 people—from every sort of church and denomination—who had come to Berth 51 in Los Angeles Harbor to see the ship arrive. Interesting that I was standing there almost as a spectator. Don had very capably brought this vision, which I had received 18 years before, to reality. This was what multiplication was all about.

Melody Green, the widow of popular singer Keith Green, recently killed in an air crash, spoke from our portable stage of Keith's great desire to see the *Anastasis* ministry launched. Then over a loudspeaker came a taped recording of Keith singing, "Holy, Holy, Holy!" As his voice filled Berth 51, our huge white ship pulled into view and steamed slowly to dockside. People picked up on Keith's theme:

> Holy, Holy, Holy,
> Lord God Almighty!
> Early in the morning,
> Our song shall rise to Thee!

I looked around me. Everywhere people were either smiling or rejoicing or weeping as they sang about the Lord. I nudged Darlene.

"What a difference," I whispered.

"Difference?"

"Between this scene, praising God the way we are, and that horrible vision nine years ago when I saw our leaders shouting in excitement over a ship but ignoring Jesus in the shadows."

"You're right," Darlene said. She took my hand. "This is what hearing God's voice is all about, isn't it? Getting to know Him better!"

Chapter Twenty

Getting to Know Him Better

It was springtime and we were in Kona. For weeks bulldozers had been rumbling over the property (to the utter delight of David, now twelve years old), rooting out boulders, leveling sites for the first buildings of Pacific and Asia Christian University.

A lot had happened in the eight months since the official welcoming there at Berth 51 in Los Angeles. The *Anastasis* had sailed to the South Pacific, helping the needy.

Our multiplication principle was strongly at work. Each of our YWAM missionaries was a potential multiplier too. Many, like Jim Rogers and Leland Paris and Floyd McClung and Don Stephens and Kalafi Moala, now headed work of their own within YWAM. It gave me the greatest satisfaction. God had multiplied the vision by thousands. Along the way, I had stumblingly learned how to hear His voice and even more stumblingly was learning to obey. Now if each of these new missionaries could do the same, using our early mistakes and successes as the stepping stones, what power would be released!

What power was *already* being released. In May 1983, our key leaders from around the world poured into Kona for our annual strategy conference. In one room were clustered some of my dearest friends, my comrades. They took turns sharing what God had been dong in their lives. We learned that . . .

- At our present rate, by December '83 YWAMers will have ministered in 193 of the 223 countries on earth.
- We will have at least 15,000 short-term volunteers go out this year.
- We will have 3,800 full-time workers by December of '83; one-fourth of these will be from the Third World.
- We will have 113 permanent bases and 70 schools located in 40 nations by the end of the year.

- We can now go with a ship full of supplies to areas where there is special need. Besides the ship's work, victims of war and poverty are being helped in 12 countries on five continents.
- In Thailand alone, YWAMers teach 700 refugee children, every day.
- Last year we gave new clothes to 30,000 refugees.
- In one year, 1,000 young evangelists from 30 different countries were sent to the Soviet Union.
- Every month YWAMers in Hollywood handle 2,000 calls from runaways, many of whom are teenage boy and girl prostitutes.

We heard how our young missionaries are going out to Himalayan kingdoms . . . up the Amazon . . . to punk rockers in Japan . . . staging street dramas in France . . . feeding Hong Kong squatters . . . helping starving African tribesmen . . . giving medical aid in Lebanon . . . and taking a Bible to every home in many Mexican cities.

As my friends told what their teams were doing in each area, I felt my excitement rising like the waves. I remembered my first trip to Africa as a young man, when I was the first missionary ever to talk to a leathery chief about the Great God who made us all. But I also recalled leaving the area by air and seeing smoke trailing upward from a thousand fires. I recalled being stunned at the enormity of the mandate *Go into all the world and preach the gospel to every creature.* Yet the smoke of African villages pales beside the multitudes of Asia, where 40,000 people can live in one high-rise apartment complex, where 60 percent of the world's people live and almost none have heard of Jesus Christ!

We send out 15,000 workers a year but they are only a fraction of what's needed. If each of these workers reached 100 people that's only one and a half million out of the four billion on earth! The laborers are still few, very few. Only God is great enough to fulfill the vision of the waves and see every person on earth receive a personal message of His love for them.

On the last evening of the strategy conference, we all went out for a dedication of the site of the university, scrambling over raw earth, roughly leveled by the bulldozers.

We stood in a circle around the site where the Plaza of

Nations would be. The sun was setting over the blue Pacific in the background. I looked at the flags of some of the nations where we were working. As they fluttered against a darkening cobalt sky, I could see the waves of young people going out. I had originally dreamed of a thousand? I could now imagine hundreds of thousands going out, until every continent, was covered by people bringing them the twin-natured message of the gospel: love the Lord with all your heart, love your neighbor as yourself.

Only one thing remained, and that would take place in just seven months.

It was Saturday morning, December 17, 1983. As the sun rose from the mountains of Hawaii, the final symbolic touchstone for our entire story was about to take place.

Darlene and I, Karen and David, Mom and Dad, and Darlene's parents were among the two thousand who were eagerly scanning the water. Small children were perched on parents' shoulders. Then, slowly, a white ship appeared on the horizon. Some started clapping. There were shouts—"Glory!" "Praise God!" Outrigger canoes hurried out to meet her as the music of a Hawaiian hymn rose above the bay.

Ten years before, when we had had the amazing experience of the Lord foretelling the future while teenagers prayed together right here in the Hawaiian Islands, we saw steaming into port a great white ship. We knew, although it defied all logic, that this somehow was going to be our Mercy Mission ship sailing into the harbor at Kona.

And here she was.

The *Anastasis*. The Resurrection. Put your dreams on the altar: they will be resurrected in something even grander.

How can I possibly explain to anyone who has not had the experience himself, the unspeakable joy of watching the Lord as He works with fallible human beings, guiding them into something as precious as this? For there was no doubt at all in my mind: what we were seeing—the university behind us and the ship in front of us—was a shout of gladness and victory from the Lord Jesus Himself.

We had at last learned the greatest of all the lessons of

guidance. It was exactly as Darlene said earlier when she took my hand and whispered:

"This is what hearing God is all about, isn't it, Loren? Getting to know Him better."

Twelve Points to Remember

Hearing the Voice of God

If you know the Lord, you have already heard His voice—it is that inner leading that brought you to Him in the first place. Jesus always checked with His Father (John 8:26–29) and so should we; hearing the voice of the heavenly Father is a basic right of every child of God. In this book we have tried to describe a few of many ways of fine-tuning this experience. The discoveries are never just theory, they come out of our own adventures:

1. Don't make guidance complicated. It's actually hard *not* to hear God if you really want to please and obey Him! If you stay humble, He promises to guide you (Proverbs 16:9).

Here are three simple steps that have helped us to hear God's voice:

- SUBMIT to His Lordship. Ask Him to help you silence your own thoughts, desires, and the opinions of others, which may be filling your mind (II Corinthians 10:5). Even though you have been given a good mind to use, right now you want to hear the thoughts of the Lord, who has the best mind (Proverbs 3:5–6).
- RESIST the enemy, in case he is trying to deceive you at this moment. Use the authority which Jesus Christ has given you to silence the voice of the enemy (James 4:7; Ephesians 6:10–20).
- EXPECT an answer. After asking the question that is on your mind, wait for Him to answer. Expect your loving heavenly Father to speak to you. He will (John 10:27; Psalm 69:13; Exodus 33:11).

2. Allow God to speak to you in the *way* He chooses. Don't try to dictate to Him concerning the guidance methods you prefer. He is Lord—you are His servant (I Samuel 3:9). So listen

with a yielded heart; there is a direct link between yieldedness and hearing. He may choose to speak to you:

Through *His Word*: this could come in your daily reading, or He could guide you to a particular verse (Psalm 119:105). Through an *audible voice* (Exodus 3:4). Through *dreams* (Matthew 2) and *visions* (Isaiah 6:1, Revelation 1:12–17). But probably the most common of all means is through the quiet, *inner voice* (Isaiah 30:21).

3. Confess any unforgiven sin. A clean heart is necessary if you want to hear God (Psalm 66:18).

4. Use The Axehead Principle—a term coined from the story in II Kings 6. If you seem to have lost your way, go back to the last time you knew the sharp, cutting edge of God's voice. Then obey. The key question is, *Have you obeyed the last thing God told you to do?*

5. Get your own leading. God will use others to confirm your guidance but you should also hear from Him directly. It can be dangerous to rely on others to get the word of the Lord for you (I Kings 13).

6. Don't talk about your guidance until God gives you permission to do so. Sometimes this happens immediately; at other times there is a delay. The main purpose of waiting is to avoid four pitfalls of guidance: (A) *pride,* because God has spoken something to you; (B) *presumption,* by speaking before you have full understanding; (C) missing God's *timing and method;* (D) bringing *confusion* to others; they too need prepared hearts (Luke 9:36; Ecclesiastes 3:7; Mark 5:19).

7. Use the Wise Men Principle. Just as the Three Wise Men individually followed the star and in doing so were all led to the same Christ, so God will often use two or more spiritually sensitive people to *confirm* what He is telling you (2 Corinthians 13:1).

8. Beware of counterfeits. Have you ever heard of a counterfeit dollar bill? Yes, of course. But have you ever heard of a counterfeit paper bag? No. The reason is, only things of value are worth counterfeiting.

Satan has a counterfeit for everything of God that is possible for him to copy (Acts 8:9–11; Exodus 7:22). Counterfeit guidance comes, for example, through ouija boards, seances, for-tunetelling, and astrology (Leviticus 20:6; 19:26; II Kings 21:6). The guidance of the Holy Spirit leads you closer to Jesus and into true freedom. Satan's guidance leads you away from God into bondage.

One key test for true guidance: does your leading follow principles of the Bible? The Holy Spirit never contradicts the Word of God.

9. Opposition of man is sometimes guidance from God (Acts 21:10–14). In our own story, we recognized much later that what seemed like blockage from our denomination was in fact God leading us into a broader scope of ministry. The important thing here, again, is *yieldedness* to the Lord (Daniel 6:6–23; Acts 4:18–21). Rebellion is never of God, but sometimes He asks you to step away from your elders in a way that is not rebellion but part of His plan. Trust that He will show your heart the difference.

10. Every follower of Jesus has a unique ministry (I Corin-thians 12; I Peter 4:10–11; Romans 12; Ephesians 4). The more you seek to hear God's voice in detail, the more effective you will be in your own calling. Guidance is not a game—it is serious business where we learn *what* God wants us to do in ministry and *how* He wants us to do it. The will of God is doing and saying the right thing in the right place, with the right people, at the right time and in the right sequence, under the right leadership, using the right method with the right attitude of heart.

11. Practice hearing God's voice and it becomes easier. It's like picking up the phone and recognizing the voice of your best friend . . . you know his voice because you have heard it so much. Compare young Samuel with the older man Samuel (I Samuel 3:4–7; 8:7–10; 12:11–18).

12. Relationship is the most important reason for hearing the voice of the Lord. God is not only infinite but personal. If you don't have communication, you don't have a personal rela-tionship with Him. True guidance, as Darlene pointed out, is getting closer to the Guide. We grow to know the Lord better as He speaks to us and, as we listen to Him and obey, we make His heart glad (Exodus 33:11, Matthew 7:24– 27).

The Work in Britain
by
LYNN GREEN

In 1970, when the School of Evangelism was underway in Switzerland, the first few YWAMers had begun to prepare the way for a Summer of Service in England. In the meantime my wife Marti and I were in the school in preparation for going to Afghanistan. On arrival there I was met with the overwhelming needs of western young people travelling east in search of religious experiences and cheap drugs. That short summer was hardly a scratch on the surface, so I decided to return the following year with a team of fifteen, which would have to be recruited in Britain. But an unexpected turn of events awaited me.

As the summer of 1971 approached, a team of fifteen were preparing to drive overland to Afghanistan, when Loren Cunningham approached Marti and me to ask us to pray about returning to England after the summer. As we sought God together, He spoke by giving us a deep desire to start a School of Evangelism similar to the one that had been so life-changing for us.

We arrived in England in 1971 with nothing but a conviction that this was where God wanted us, and a vision that God's Spirit could move across this land. We came empty handed, without resources, and with little support, but in another sense we came with arms full of the promises of a loving and faithful God.

Through the past fourteen years God has continually proved Himself worthy of our allegiance. A graphic example of God's faithfulness in leading us in the early stages of the work here is the story of how we obtained our first base in England.

We knew God was saying that if we were obedient He would enable us to purchase a place in which we could run a School of Evangelism. Somehow in our hearts, we knew that it needed to be in central West Sussex. In December of 1971 we saw it. A house called Holmsted Manor. My first reaction was that it was too big. I was thinking of a school with thirty students at most; this place would house a hundred! But as I walked in through the front door with the estate agent, God spoke, not with audible words, but with a strong inner sense that I belonged here. A few weeks later we prayed about it with Loren, who said, "Remember, God is more interested in building a man of God through this than in the building itself."

Though we had only about £200 towards purchasing Holmsted, we began to pray and believe that God would provide it as a training base. We prayed and waited several months, but nothing seemed to happen. Then we heard rumours that the owner was about to sell it to a property developer. We knew he surely couldn't because God had promised it to us. What confusion we experienced when we found it had indeed been sold!

Further prayer followed and we began to learn that faith is based on the promises of God, not on circumstances. We still believed for Holmsted. Several months later, in late 1972, I experienced a strong desire to drive from London down to Holmsted Manor, just to see it. Somehow I thought it might be for sale again. I was almost over-whelmed with excitement when I saw the For Sale sign. Later that same day my joy turned to dismay when I found the price had trebled.

During this time, we were living in a small house in London, and our housing needs became more pressing month by month as more people joined us in the work of evangelism and training. Eventually we had forty-two people with us, and only one bathroom! Virtually every room in the house was turned into a bedroom.

Then God began to provide financially. A number of people in the south of England became aware of our housing needs, and began to give selflessly and generously. Though quite a lot of money was given it only amounted to about the original asking price for Holmsted, and the new owners were confident that they had a buyer at the new inflated price. We expected that any day they would become more agreeable, but they didn't. Once again it was sold.

Though God graciously provided temporary accommodation for us we still had the grace to believe for what He had promised. We simply carried on with the work of training and evangelism.

In December 1974 we began to hear rumours that Holmsted was coming up for sale again. By February 1975 the For Sale sign went up. Due to a sudden slump in the property market the price of it had dropped. After several weeks of spiritual battle and negotiations God completed His four-year miracle and we bought Holmsted Manor for the original price.

Through those years God did use it, as Loren said, to teach us many of His ways: to persist in prayer; to believe His Word even when circumstances don't seem to confirm it; to get on with ministering to people, not diverting our energies into material things; and to do everything to the glory of God.

Since 1976 Holmsted Manor has been a wonderful home for our training schools. Many hundreds of people have been trained to be disciples of the Lord Jesus Christ, and are now living for Him in different places throughout the world.

From the humble beginnings when there were just the two of us, we have seen God's blessing as Loren's vision became realized in the UK. We now have a staff of nearly 250, individuals from all across the globe committed to seeing God's kingdom spread throughout these islands. In addition to the full-time workers there are some 3,000 more individuals involved in our ministry through their unfailing interest, prayers, support and love. It would take another book, the same size as this one, to trace the work of God as He has multiplied and matured the vision and ministry of YWAM in this country and to give recognition to all those thousands who have played a part in the work. Here I will attempt to give a brief outline of the ministries God has led us into as we have been obedient to His voice.

Evangelism

YWAM began with Loren's vision of mobilizing young people to effectively share the gospel across the world. This remains a vital task. Every summer large numbers of people from England and abroad attend a blitz course on evangelism and are then sent out in teams to key locations in the London area and other major cities across the country. These teams, often one hundred or more strong, participate in all sorts of evangelism, such as street drama, street preaching, one-to-one witnessing and coffee-bar ministry. Through these Summer of Service times each year the gospel is effectively conveyed to thousands, many who have never heard the good news before. In

London, during the course of one summer week, team members may witness to people from scores of nations, many of which are closed to the gospel. Many involved in these outreaches have never verbally shared their faith with non-believers. After the Summer of Service they return to their homes, jobs and churches, eager to continue proclaiming the love of God.

Throughout the rest of the year, both local and travelling teams continue evangelistic work with local churches, Christian Unions and youth groups across the country. These teams stimulate evangelism through training seminars and participating in local evangelistic outreaches.

TRAINING

It was in the mid-seventies that God was showing Loren and other leaders that evangelism alone was not enough. We discovered Christians often lacked training in basic biblical principles of how to live the victorious Christian life. God showed us that it is the application of such principles which empowers our daily witness. Following God's direction we began training programmes that would assist Christians to know God and thereby make Him known to others. We now run Discipleship Training Schools in our bases in Holmsted Manor, the Kings Lodge near Nuneaton and the Overtoun House outside Glasgow. These five-month courses provide practical teaching which has Christlikeness as its goal. Each course includes one to two months of outreach, often in a foreign land. This period of intense evangelism is a time in which the students live out the principles they have learned during the lecture phase.

Through the years other training programmes have developed to aid in the equipping of the saints. At week-long seminars we are able to share principles studied at the Discipleship Training Schools with those who are unable to spend five months away from home or job. Seminars on leadership have proved fruitful in equipping individuals for leadership roles in the local church. Mobile teams are able to take training to churches and other Christian groups across the nation. Other teams such as the Dilaram House in South East London concentrate on bringing new converts to maturity, many being street people who are not yet ready to mix in a church fellowship.

The future holds opportunities for numerous new training programmes to meet the needs of a changing world. A School of Evangelism will prepare long-term workers for cross-cultural and urban missions. A School of Biblical Studies and a School of Biblical Counselling are projects we look forward to which will further equip Christians for more specialized service in the church.

MERCY MINISTRIES

In recent years there has been a new emphasis in YWAM as God has continued to mature us as a mission. Mercy ministry, reaching out to those in need, is becoming more and more a focus in our work in Britain and abroad. Jesus spent the majority of his time with the oppressed, the poor and the outcast. We must follow his example. Homelessness, drug addiction and poverty are a few of the growing problems across our land. Through mercy ministries we are taking practical action, identifying and meeting some of these needs that threaten to overwhelm us.

Across the globe YWAM is involved in medical assistance, building and maintenance, literacy work, and feeding and clothing the needy. Among refugees in Thailand, orphans in Colombia, and the destitute of London we are reaching out, proclaiming the gospel in deed that we might better proclaim it in word.

YWAM Great Britain is still in its growing stages. God continues to lead us and guide us, maturing us as a mission. The vision that spurred us on in the early seventies has not faded; it has widened and sharpened. New possibilities, new potential awaits YWAM as we work with the rest of the community of the faithful to spread the kingdom of God to all the world.

For further information about Youth With A Mission in Great Britain, please write to:

Youth With A Mission
Holmsted Manor
Staplefield Road
Cuckfield
West Sussex RH17 5JF